THE BEST
MUSIC
THEORY
BOOK
FOR BEGINNERS

A Guide for Everyone:
How to Read, Write, and Understand Music

How this Series Works

Read = write + understand most modern music ⟶ **Level 3**

Level 2

You are here ⟶ **Level 1**

STOP

ISBN: 978-1-957835-03-7

@bestmusiccoach
www.bestmusiccoach.com
facebook.com/bestmusiccoach
youtube.com/bestmusiccoach
twitter.com/bestmusiccoach
instagram.com/bestmusiccoach

Book Design by Adam Hay Studio
Diagrams and Illustrations by Arron Leishman

Enhance Your Understanding + Learn Fast!
Get The Music Theory Workbook Now!

Welcome to Best Music Coach!

learn the rules, follow the rules, break the rules, make music. the music in your heart may not conform to the rules you will learn in this book, or it may follow the rules without exception. rules provide a structure to be creative in. all ways of making music are fine. go make music and express yourself with passion.

A note to adult students and parents of younger students

It is my sincere goal to make every page of this book worth your time. I will do everything to empower you to get where you want to go...your dream music goal.

My passion is sharing everything I have learned along the way of two college degrees, professional experience in guitar, singing, songwriting, (a little) producing, and teaching.

I wrote this book for you because I failed to test out of an easy 101 class at my second college. Yes, that means I failed a 101 class while having a degree in music (sad face). I pulled myself back from embarrassing failure by finding easier ways of understanding how music works. By my last semester, I was the first to turn in class assignments...I understood music so deeply music theory became as easy as breathing. The hacks, tips, and tricks that I used on myself and tested on hundreds of students are now in your hands!

This book is for all instruments, singers, songwriters, producers, DJs, composers, music students, and anyone who is interested in understanding more about music.

The goal of this book? To make it easy for you to apply the music theory knowledge to composing, songwriting, your instrument, singing, and music production.

You will own the foundation for modern and classical music, including all types of pop, punk, metal, CCM, rock, hip-hop, funk, blues, rock 'n' roll, musical theater, jazz, fusion, folk, classical music from all periods and many, many other genres and styles of music.

You are now officially a **Music Maker**. Yes, even if you have never played, sang, written, or produced a single note. You are stepping into your music journey. You are a **Music Maker.**

Welcome.

Let's do this.

Dan Spencer
Lead Coach

I am here for you.
Get free lessons and community
facebook.com/groups/musicmakersofficial

Contents

How to Scan QR Codes

1

2

3

1. On an iPhone, open the camera. On an Android, download and open a QR code-scanner application.

2. Hold your phone so you can see the QR code on the screen, with the screen in focus.

3. On iPhones, tap the banner that asks you if you want to open the QR code. On Android, tap the button that asks you to open the QR code. Give it a try with the QR code below this writing!

Claim your FREE course with easy bite-sized lessons guide you through this book so you can learn faster. Scan the code to claim your FREE Gifts now!

Music Theory: Introduction

What Is Music Theory?

The study and understanding of the elements and structure of music. It is the key to understanding the "how" and the "why" behind all music you hear or play.

Why Learn Music Theory?

Learn Pieces of Music Faster on Any Instrument or Voice

Just like using a GPS app will get to your destination faster, music theory shows you the way to the end of a piece of music, speeding memorization, because you understand what is actually going on. With this, you will be able to play and sing music more accurately, with a deeper intellectual and emotional understanding and interpretation.

Get Better at Writing Music

Anytime you write songs (songwriting), compositions (composing), or produce music (music production), you are using music theory. You now have a clear path to easily use music theory to create. There is even a chapter dedicated to take everything you learn here and use it to write music. Writing and creating music is a journey, and this is the **first step**.

Strengthen Your Relationship to All the Music in Your Life

Music theory will help you understand and relate to all music you hear.

What You Will Need

1. This book.

2. Manuscript paper.

3. Pencils.

4. A ruler (optional, but recommended for writing by hand).

5. The workbook. Music theory is like anything. Use it or lose it.

Scan the code below for my recommendations.

How This Book Works

Free Audio and Video Examples and Flashcards

This book comes with video examples of exercises and songs. Any time you see the icon (23) it is showing the video example number for you to listen to or watch to help you understand the song or exercise. All video examples can be found by scanning the QR code below with your device or at

bestmusiccoach.com/books

1. Click on "Music Theory."

2. Click on "The Best Music Theory Books for Beginners **Series.**"

3. Click on "The Best Music Theory Books for Beginners **1.**"

4. Click on "Free Examples" then create a free account—click "Login to Enroll."

Workbook Sync

This book syncs up with a workbook. Every time **a concept in this book** is linked with activities in the workbook, you will find a matching number in a light bulb 💡 in this book and next to the connected activities in your *Best Music Theory Workbook 1*, 3rd edition.

How to Read Timestamps

The timestamp shows how many seconds or minutes into music examples begin, and when it ends.

03:29 – 05:00
minutes:seconds   minutes:seconds

Example starts at three minutes   Example ends at five minutes
and twenty-nine seconds   and zero seconds

Rhythm 1: How to Understand, Write, and Perform Notes

Whether playing an instrument, singing, or creating music, a solid grasp of rhythm paves the way for musical expression, creativity, and connecting with others through the language of music.

① Rhythm

- Rhythm is sound grouped into patterns.
- The patterns are made through sound and silence.
- Rhythm is like a light bulb — it is either on or off. On is sound, off is silence.
- Rhythm can be:
  Fast
  Slow
  Loud
  Quiet
  Rhythm can speed up
  Rhythm can slow down

Pulse

② Pulse: Sound

Pulse is a type of rhythm, and is a group of identical sounds that repeat at the same volume and speed.

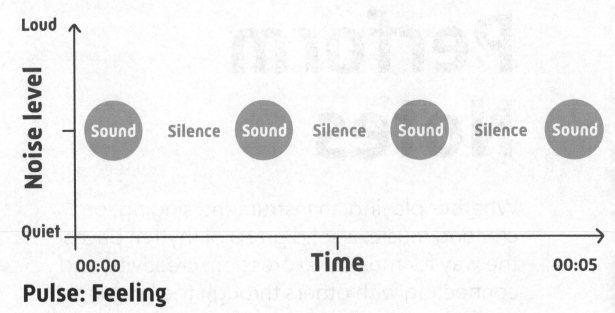

Pulse: Feeling

The word pulse also means the subjective underlying rhythm of music that you feel but can't see or write down. Different people can feel a pulse in different ways for the same music!

1. Listen to any pop music and clap your hands along with it.

2. You are most likely clapping along with a pulse.

3. Someone else might clap two times faster or slower than you!

③ Beat

- A beat is a type of rhythm.

- A beat is counted at the even speed of a particular pulse in the music. When this happens, a beat is then called "the beat" (more on this later; move forward for now).

- A beat is different from a pulse because it can be loud or quiet and does not have to sound the same all the time.

- A beat is made with many pulses that are different from one another.

- In a beat, more than one pulse can sound at a time.

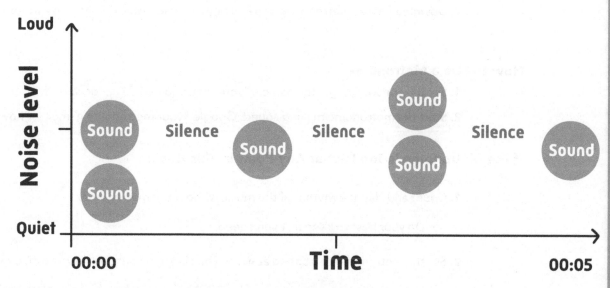

Other Uses of the Word Beat

1. Used to describe a particular pulse. Example: "Can you feel the beat?"

2. Instrumental music for hip-hop or pop music that is used for singers or rappers to record and perform with is sometimes called a "beat."

The Metronome

A metronome is a device or app that produces a pulse sound called a "click" that you can speed up or slow down. We measure music speed by how many click sounds the metronome makes every minute, called "beats per minute" (BPM) because the beat is the same speed as the metronome pulse sound.

> **metronome click sound = beat**

Metronome Speed Icon

The speed at which you should complete clapping examples looks like this: **60** .
This means: set a metronome to 60 BPM and start it making sound before you start the example.

Where to Get a Metronome

> **1.** Search "metronome" in the App Store (iPhone) or Google Play (Android).
>
> **2.** Download a free metronome. You can buy a physical one. Google "metronome buy."

How to Use a Metronome

> **1.** Set the speed. Google the name of your metronome + "change speed."
>
> **2.** Start the metronome making sound. Google "your metronome name" + "how use."

If the Metronome Is Too Fast at Any Point in This Book:

> **1.** Count and clap the rhythm of the music without the metronome.
>
> • Do your best to keep an even speed.
>
> **2.** Set the metronome to a speed at which you clap and count the music with 0 mistakes.
>
> • Increase the metronome speed by 5 BPM. If you make a mistake, slow back down.
>
> • Continue increasing by 5 BPM each repetition until you can clap the example at the suggested speed with 0 mistakes. If you make a mistake, slow back down.

There are three types of metronome:

Digital Metronome   **Software Metronome on a Phone**   **Mechanical/Electromechanical**

Count In

The count in is giving the beat with spoken words or sounds. This is like: "On your mark, get set, go!" so musicians can start making music at the same time and speed together. The beginning of the following songs feature a count in.

LISTEN

I Saw Her Standing There	The Beatles
Patience	Guns N' Roses
Hey Ya!	Outkast

Count In: Application

Give yourself a count in before performing the exercises in this book or your own compositions.

(4) **Count In: Four**

1. Listen to the metronome until you can hear the pattern and anticipate when the next click will happen before moving forward. When you feel you can anticipate the timing between the clicks:

2. Count "1, 2, 3, 4" aloud with each number you speak happening at the same time as a click. This is "counting the beat."

3. Try to be as precise as possible and speak exactly with the clicking sound, not before or after.

(5) **Count In: Three**

1. Listen to the metronome until you can hear the pattern and anticipate when the next click will happen before moving forward. When you feel you can anticipate the timing between the clicks:

2. Count "1, 2, 3" aloud with each number you speak happening at the same time as a click. This is "counting the beat."

3. Try to be as precise as possible and speak exactly with the clicking sound, not before or after.

Tempo/Time/Speed

"Tempo" is an Italian word that means "time." We use tempo to mean the speed of music. The correct plural of tempo is "tempi," but many musicians say and write "tempos."

Example: The tempos of all three awesome songs you wrote in 10 minutes flat using what you learned from this book are 80 BPM, 77 BPM, and 120 BPM.

Tempo Examples 1

Slow	"At Last"	Etta James
Medium	"Ho Hey"	The Lumineers
Fast	"September"	Earth, Wind & Fire

Tempo Examples 2

Slow	"A Change Is Gonna Come"	Sam Cooke
Medium	"Jump Start"	Greg Howe
Fast	"Love Is a Battlefield"	Pat Benatar

> The medium sounds fast in Tempo Examples 2. Learn what makes these songs fast or slow in a few pages!

Lines

Music is written on lines — either a single line or the staff, which is five parallel lines. You will see both single and the group of five lines in this book. The group of five parallel lines is called the "staff."

Single line

_____

Staff (five parallel lines)

_____
_____
_____
_____
_____

Notes

Musicians play, read, and write rhythm with symbols called "notes." These are three types of noteheads for notes. Two of the noteheads also have vertical "stems."

open notehead (whole note)   **open notehead (half note)**   **closed notehead (quarter note)**

stem   stem

> The different notes show how long a sound will last. A note's duration is called "rhythmic value." A whole note has a larger rhythmic value than a quarter note, so it lasts longer.

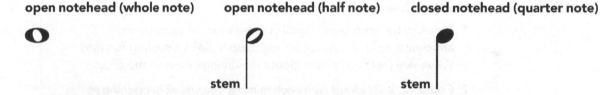

1 whole note = Long duration.
One whole note lasts for four counts/beats.

1   **2**   **3**   **4**

= 2 half notes = Medium duration.
One half note lasts for two counts/beats.

1   **2**   **3**   **4**

= 4 quarter notes = Short duration.
One quarter note lasts for one count/beat.

1   **2**   **3**   **4**

How to Write Whole, Half, and Quarter Notes

 ## The Staff: Lines and Spaces

On the staff there are 5 lines and 4 spaces between the lines. Each line and space has a number so we can name lines and spaces without saying things like "the fourth line from the top." That's "Line 2."

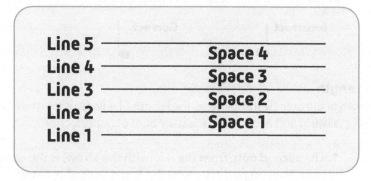

How to Write Noteheads

Closed Noteheads

Closed noteheads are a tilted oval.

Open Noteheads: Half Notes

Open noteheads for half notes are a tilted oval shape with no center.

Open Noteheads: Whole Notes

Open noteheads for whole notes are oval with no center and are **not** tilted.

In a Space

Each notehead in a space touches the lines above and below the space without going over either line. The hollow center of open noteheads goes in the middle of the space. **Note in space = stay in space**

On a Line

The notehead does not touch the lines above or below it. There is space above and below the notehead so anyone can see it is touching one line only. You should be able to see the line of the staff and space around it in the middle of open noteheads. **Note on line = only touch one line**

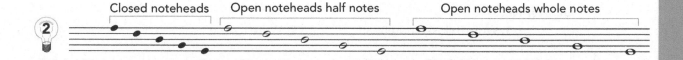

How to Write Stems

Stems and Noteheads

1. Notes with a stem down look like a letter p.

Incorrect   **Correct**

2. Notes with a stem up look like a letter d.

Incorrect   **Correct**

Stem Length

The length of the stem is the same as the length of 4 lines of the staff. Do your best to keep the stem lengths consistent and accept a modest amount of imperfection.

1. The second note from the left (with the arrow) is the easiest example to see because the stem lines up perfectly with the first 4 lines of the staff.

2. All the other notes also have stems that are four staff lines long, too.

Stem Direction: Stem Down
On or above Line 3 of the staff

Stem Direction: Stem Up
Below Line 3 of the staff

How to Write Whole, Half, and Quarter Notes

Whole Notes
    1. Write an open notehead.

Half Notes
    1. Write an open notehead.   **2.** Write a stem.

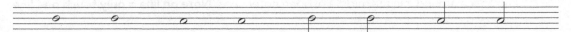

Quarter Notes
    1. Write a closed notehead.   **2.** Write a stem.

How to Clap Rhythms

You can rock, sway, and move your body with the click of the metronome (*it helps some people*).

> **Reminder:** You can start without the metronome or slow the metronome down if you need to. Give yourself a count in of "1, 2, 3, 4" along with the metronome before starting these exercises.

Key: Clap Hands = ↑   Count = count aloud

How to Clap Quarter Notes

1. Clap on every beat (on every click) of the metronome. These are quarter notes.

2. Be precise as possible and clap exactly with the clicking sound, not before or after.

3. When this is comfortable, repeat "1, 2, 3, 4" aloud over and over again, with one number per clap. Speak and clap exactly with the click. You are counting the beat!

How to Clap Half Notes

1. Clap on beat 1, skip beat 2, clap on beat 3, and skip beat 4.

2. Continue clapping every other beat.

3. Count "1, 2, 3, 4" aloud as you clap. You are counting the beat!

How to Clap Whole Notes

1. Clap beat 1, then do not clap on beats 2, 3, 4.

2. You should be clapping once every 4 beats.

3. Add in the "1, 2, 3, 4" count. You are counting the beat!

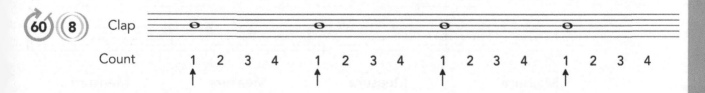

Why Clap?

We clap because it is much easier than playing an instrument. We clap because it helps you learn how the rhythm of the music sounds and works at a deeper level than writing.

How to Clap Fast

Touch the palms of your hands together. If you are right-handed: with your right hand on top, keep your left hand flat and still and clap by only moving your right hand with your wrist. If you are left-handed: left hand on top, keep your right hand flat and still and clap by only moving your left hand with your wrist.

Bar Lines and Their Meanings

Bar lines divide groups of notes.

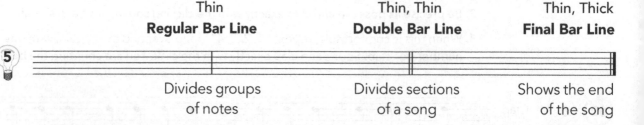

Thin	Thin, Thin	Thin, Thick
Regular Bar Line	**Double Bar Line**	**Final Bar Line**
Divides groups of notes	Divides sections of a song	Shows the end of the song

> **Pieces of Music vs. Songs**
> A "piece" can have a singer and words or only instruments. Songs must have words and a singer. In classical, cinematic, and video game music there are pieces with singers that are not songs.
>
> **singer = song (a lot of the time)   no words = piece**

Measures

A measure is a space on a staff where notes and other notation are placed. Each measure touches bar lines. For this reason, some people call measures "bars." The beat count restarts every measure.

- **m.** is the abbreviation of the word "measure."
- **mm.** is the abbreviation of the word "measures."
- The first measure has only one bar line.

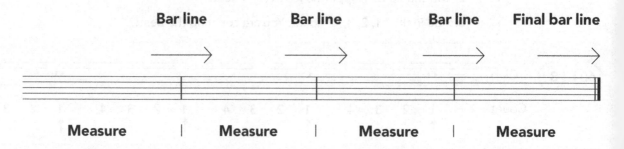

Bar line	Bar line	Bar line	Final bar line

| Measure | Measure | Measure | Measure |

Measures of 4

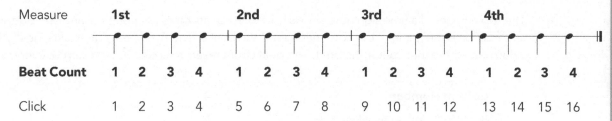

Measure	1st				2nd				3rd				4th			
Beat Count	1	2	3	4	1	2	3	4	1	2	3	4	1	2	3	4
Click	1	2	3	4	5	6	7	8	9	10	11	12	13	14	15	16

Measures of 3

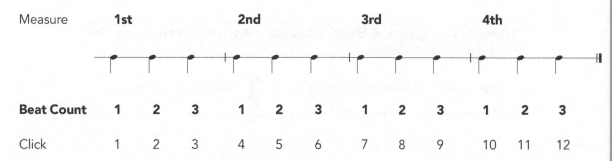

Measure	1st			2nd			3rd			4th		
Beat Count	1	2	3	1	2	3	1	2	3	1	2	3
Click	1	2	3	4	5	6	7	8	9	10	11	12

What Is an "Attack" in Music?

Whenever you clap a note or start any sound it is called an "attack." This word may seem aggressive, but is correct for playing music, and is in the dictionary.

Attack. noun. the act or manner of beginning a musical note.

*MUSIC MAKERS...**ATTACK!** (haha)*

Composer vs. Songwriter

Composer. noun. a person who writes music.

Songwriter. noun. a person who writes music and lyrics for songs.

Composers and songwriters can be different, just like pieces of music and songs. Songwriters typically write songs that have words (lyrics). Composers don't write music with lyrics all the time.

In professional circles, composers write more formal or complex music and songwriters write songs in modern genres like pop or rock. Neither is better or worse; they are just different.

Are you a composer or songwriter when you create your music? It doesn't matter. Create music that you are passionate about and let the rest of the world figure out how to categorize you.

Time Signatures

The top number of a time signature shows how many beats there are per measure. The bottom number as a fraction is the name of the note that "gets" the beat count. Each beat count lasts the rhythmic value of the note that "gets" the beat. The beat count resets to count 1 at the start of every measure.

Bottom Number	4
Bottom Number as a Fraction	¼
Name of the Fraction	Quarter
Note Value that Gets the Beat/Count	Quarter note
The Beat Count Lines Up With The	Quarter note

When a note "gets the beat" it lines up with a beat count number.

Top: Number of beats per measure?   4/4   Four beats per measure.

Bottom: Which type of note gets the beat?   4/4   Quarter note "gets" the beat.

Measures of 3

beats per measure

3/4

quarter note gets the beat

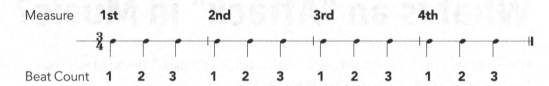

Measures of 4

beats per measure

4/4

quarter note gets the beat

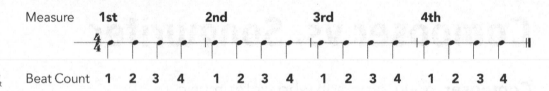

Because of its popularity and common use (it is used a lot), 4/4 can be written as "common time."

💡6   4/4 = 𝐂 = common time

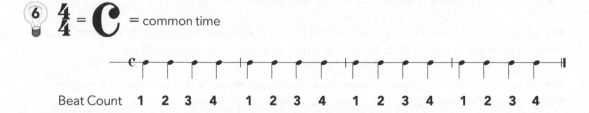

Percussion Clef

The percussion clefs shows that only rhythm will happen in the music written on a single line or 5-line staff. The percussion clef is also called a "neutral clef."

What Is a Clef?

A clef is a symbol on the left-hand side of a staff that shows how notes written on the staff will sound.

⑦ How to Write a Percussion Clef

Write two vertical lines from the 4th line of the staff to the 2nd line of the staff. Make the lines thick.

In $\frac{3}{4}$ the count in is 1, 2, 3.

Clap and Count 1

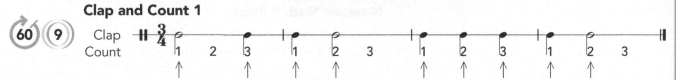

Clap and Count 2

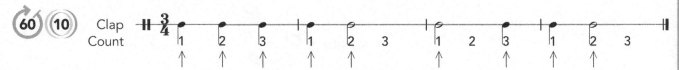

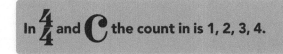

In $\frac{4}{4}$ and $\mathbf{C}$ the count in is 1, 2, 3, 4.

Clap and Count 3

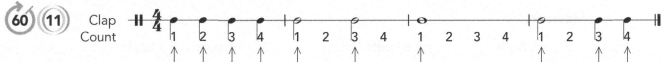

Clap and Count 4

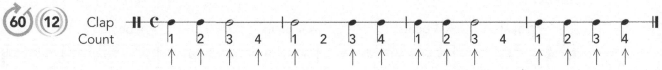

How to Write Music 1

When you write music, you are doing one of three things.

1. Creating something brand new — original songs and compositions

This is called composing or songwriting. This is when you create original combinations of notes in your measures.

2. Completing an exercise

Like using *The Best Music Theory Workbook 1.*

3. Copying another piece of music

This is called transcribing. You can transcribe music that you hear or copy other written music.

Measure Math 1

Measure Math 1 Rules:
Every measure must add up to the number of beats in the top number of the time signature.

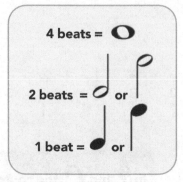

Measure Math 4/4

Each measure in the incorrect example contains note values that do not add up to 4 beat counts. In the correct example, every measure contains note values that add up to 4 beat counts.

Incorrect

Correct

Measure Math 3/4

Each measure in the incorrect example contains note values that do not add up to 3 beat counts. In the correct example, every measure contains note values that add up to 3 beat counts.

Incorrect

Correct

How to Write Lines of Music 1

> ### How to Write a Line of Four Measures
>
> **1.** Divide the line of staff in half vertically with a single bar line.
>
> **2.** Divide the staff into quarters with two more bar lines with extra space in the first measure for a clef and time signature.
>
> **3.** Write a final bar line (the thick line is 4-6 times thicker than the thin line), percussion clef, and time signature. The top number of the time signature takes up the space from Line 3 to 5. The bottom number of the time signature takes up the space from Line 1 to 3.
>
> **4.** Write notes to fill each measure with the number of beats shown in the time signature.

A "line of staff" is all 5 lines of the staff together.

1.

2.

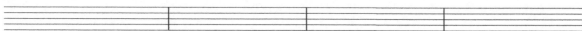

3.

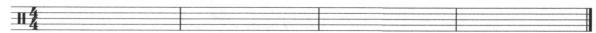

4.

How to Write Whole Notes, Half Notes, and Quarter Notes in a Measure

Use this page as a quick reference for writing your first compositions or songs.

How to Write Music in $\frac{4}{4}$

1. Every measure must add up to 4 beats.

2. Notes end inside the measure they start in; they can't cross measure lines.

3. Whole notes can only be written on beat 1.

4. Half notes can be written on beats 1, 2, and 3.

5. Quarter notes can be written on beats 1, 2, 3, and 4.

6. Set up a line of staff with a percussion clef and time signature in $\frac{4}{4}$.

7. Write 4 beats worth of notes in each measure.

How to Write Music in $\frac{3}{4}$

1. Every measure must add up to 3 beats.

2. Notes end inside the measure they start in; they can't cross measure lines.

3. A whole note cannot be written in $\frac{3}{4}$. This is because the whole note gets four beats, and each measure in $\frac{3}{4}$ can only hold three beats in total.

4. Half notes can be written on beats 1 and 2.

5. Quarter notes can be written on beats 1, 2, and 3.

6. Set up a line of staff with a percussion clef and time signature in $\frac{3}{4}$.

7. Write 3 beats worth of notes in each measure.

Measure Math 1 Rules:

1. Every measure must add up to the number of beats in the top number of the time signature.

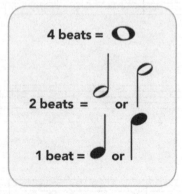

How to Write and Perform Your Own Music!

Writing your own music is a joyful opportunity to share and express your thoughts, feelings, emotions, and ideas. The better you know the fundamentals like writing notes and measure math, the sooner you will be free to focus on creation, creativity, and expression.

> **How to Create and Perform Your Own Song or Composition in 3/4 and 4/4**
> 1. Pick a line or space on the staff.
> 2. Create music in 3/4 or 4/4.
> 3. Check your noteheads.
> 4. Check your stem lengths.
> 5. Check your measure math.
> 6. Add the beat count below the staff.
> 7. (Optional) Add clapping arrows.
> 8. Clap and count your music with a metronome.

Original Composition Example

Note Spacing

Each note lines up with a beat. Measures are divided into equal parts to help us "see" the rhythmic value of notes.

4 beats per measure = 4 divisions
3 beats per measure = 3 divisions

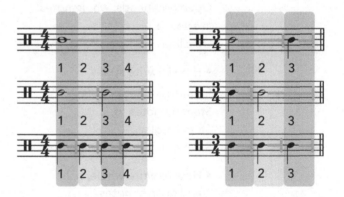

Correct

Incorrect

Review: Rhythm 1

- Rhythm

- Pulse

Pulse: sound

Pulse: feeling

- Beat

- The metronome

- Count in

- Tempo/Time

- Lines

Single line

Staff (five lines)

- Notes

Whole notes

Half notes

Quarter notes

- The staff: lines and spaces

- How to write noteheads

Closed noteheads

Open noteheads: half notes

Open noteheads: whole notes

In a space

On a line

- How to write stems

Stem-down notes: p

Stem-up notes: d

Stem length

Stem direction

- How to write whole, half, and quarter notes

- How to clap notes

Quarter notes

Half notes

Whole notes

Why we clap

How to clap fast

- Bar lines and their meanings

Regular bar line

Double bar line

Final bar line

New Words You Should Know

1. Rhythm
2. Pulse
3. Beat
4. Metronome
5. Tempo
6. Staff
7. Notehead
8. Stem
9. Bar line
10. Measure
11. Attack
12. Time signature
13. Clef

- Measures

m. = measure

mm. = measures

- What is an "attack" in music?

- Composer vs. songwriter

- Time signatures

When a note get the beat it gets the count

- Percussion clef

- How to write music 1

Measure math

How to write lines of music

How to write whole notes, half notes, and quarter notes in a measure

How to write and perform your own compositions

Rhythm 2: Strong and Weak Beats 1

Changing between strong and weak beats shapes the way music flows. This creates a framework that we can use to understand many parts of music.

Strong and Weak Beats

In every measure of all time signatures there are stronger and weaker beats. This is part of what gives music life. If all beats were equally strong, they would not be beats — they would be a pulse. Alternating strong and weak beats gives music momentum and movement. Just like the beat count, the pattern of strong and weak beats repeat every measure.

Why Are Some Beats Strong and Some Beats Weak?

Stronger and weaker beats change how music is played, written, understood, and performed. Together as a European/Western music culture, we have agreed that certain beats get more emphasis than others. Every time signature has its own series of stronger and weaker beats.

Strong and Weak Beat Colors

To help identify the strong and weak beats, use the color system below.

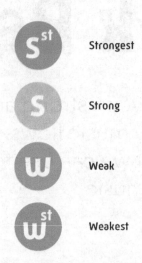

Sst   Strongest

S   Strong

W   Weak

Wst   Weakest

Strong and Weak Beat Colors 4/4

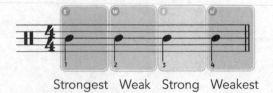

Strongest   Weak   Strong   Weakest

Strong and Weak Beat Colors 3/4

Strongest   Weak   Weakest

The Power of Low Sounds

The natural human tendency is to perceive lower sounds as being more important and more powerful than higher sounds. In many modern music genres, the strongest beats in the measure will have lower-sounding instruments on the strongest and strong beats to help emphasize them.

Strong and Weak Beats: Drums

Since there is a drum set (or digital/analog equivalent) in most songs, you will understand strong and weak beats through listening to recordings of drum kits and reading the notation.

Drum Kit Basics

1 **Snare drum:** the loudest, but higher sounding drum. The snare will sound on weaker beats.

2 **Kick drum:** the lowest-sounding drum. The kick will sound on the strongest beats. Kick drum quarter notes are stem down below Line 3 of the staff, an exception to the "stem down from Line 3 up" rule.

(13) **1** **Snare: Weak & Weakest Beats**

(14) **2** **Kick: Strongest & Strong Beats**

Snare + Kick 4/4

Snare + Kick 3/4

Strong and Weak Beats: 4/4

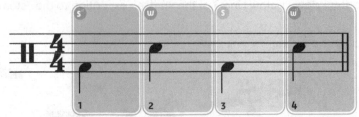

Measure	1 Measure			
Beats	Beat 1	Beat 2	Beat 3	Beat 4
Strength	Strongest	Weak	Strong	Weakest
Snare	Silent	Play	Silent	Play
Kick	Play	Silent	Play	Silent

How to Identify Time Signatures by Ear: 4/4

1. Listen to the recordings listed below and try to focus on the kick drum and snare only.

2. Sometimes the snare pattern will vary. In general, listen for the snare on the weak and weakest beats.

3. Sometimes the kick pattern will vary. In general, listen for the kick on the strongest and strong beats.

4. To confirm the time signature, count "1, 2, 3, 4" along with the music and try to align that count with a pulse that you can feel.

Example:

This kick drum pattern can be heard in **"We Didn't Start the Fire"** by Billy Joel (00:14–00:39) and **"Into the Great Wide Open"** by Tom Petty and the Heartbreakers (00:49–01:09). Kick drum patterns get much more complex than this, but this is a good place to start.

LISTEN

"Dream On"	Aerosmith
"Roll Over Beethoven"	Chuck Berry
"Crazy in Love"	Beyoncé feat. Jay-Z
"Livin' on a Prayer"	Bon Jovi
"Bye Bye Love"	The Everly Brothers
"The Chain"	Fleetwood Mac
"Ain't Nobody"	Chaka Khan and Rufus
"My Sharona"	The Knack
"Seasons of Love"	Jonathan Larson
"I'm Yours"	Jason Mraz
"Purple Rain"	Prince
"Losing My Religion"	R.E.M.
"Helpless"	Neil Young

Strong and Weak Beats: $\frac{3}{4}$

$\frac{3}{4}$

Measure	1 Measure		
Beats	Beat 1	Beat 2	Beat 3
Strength	Strongest	Weak	Weakest
Snare	Silent	Play	Play
Kick	Play	Silent	Silent

How to Identify Time Signatures by Ear: $\frac{3}{4}$

1. Listen to the recordings listed below and try to focus on the kick drum and snare only.

2. Sometimes the snare pattern will vary. In general, listen for the snare on the weak and weakest beats.

3. Sometimes the kick pattern will vary. In general, listen for the kick on the strongest beat.

4. To confirm the time signature, count "1, 2, 3" along with the music and try to align that count with a pulse that you can feel.

A few of these examples do not have drums, or only have drums in part of the song. Uh oh! What to do? Listen for the pattern of strong, weak, weakest. The strong and weak beats are something we have agreed on in our music culture, and they show up everywhere in all instruments!

10 LISTEN

"Sing It Again"	Beck
"Hickory Wind"	The Byrds
"Sunday's Best"	Elvis Costello and The Attractions
"Que Sera, Sera"	Doris Day
"The Times They Are A-Changin'"	Bob Dylan
"Manic Depression"	Jimi Hendrix
"(How Much Is) That Doggie in the Window?"	Patti Page
"No Other One"	Weezer
"La Bohème"	Charles Aznavour

Remember back on p. 13 how it was difficult to tell which songs were faster or slower? Use your new knowledge of strong and weak beats and listen to the drums in those songs to hear where the actual beats are!

Review: Rhythm 2

- Strong and weak beat culture
- Strong and weak beat colors

 Strongest

 Strong

 Weak

 Weakest

- Strong and weak beats in $\frac{4}{4}$

- Strong and weak beats in $\frac{3}{4}$

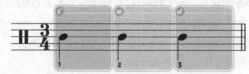

- The power of low sounds
- Strong and weak beats: drums

  Snare

  Kick

- Strong and weak beats: $\frac{4}{4}$

  How to identify time signatures by ear

Claim your FREE course with easy bite-sized lessons guide you through this book so you can learn faster. Scan the code to claim your FREE Gifts now!

Rhythm 3: How to Understand, Write, and Perform Rests

Rests are musical symbols that show silence instead of sound. Reading and writing rests empowers you to bring depth, precision, and expressive nuance to understanding, creating, and performing music.

Rests

Rests are musical notations that show silence for a certain number of beats counts.

- Rests are silent.

- Count them. Don't clap them.

- Perform an "anti-clap" on rests. Move your dominant clapping hand fingers up, away from your other hand keeping palms touching.

- Whole rests are equal to whole notes in duration.

- Half rests are equal to half notes in duration.

- Quarter rests are equal to quarter notes in duration.

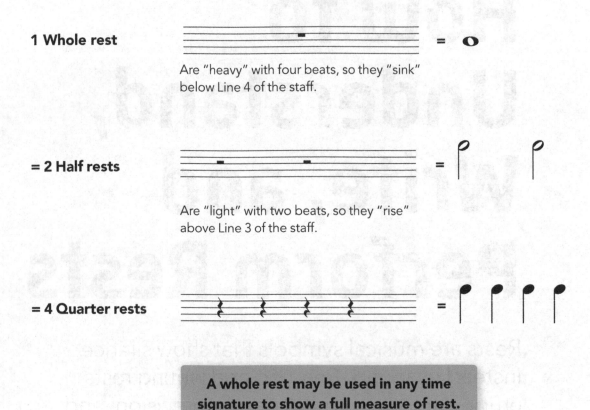

1 Whole rest

Are "heavy" with four beats, so they "sink" below Line 4 of the staff.

= 2 Half rests

Are "light" with two beats, so they "rise" above Line 3 of the staff.

= 4 Quarter rests

> **A whole rest may be used in any time signature to show a full measure of rest.**

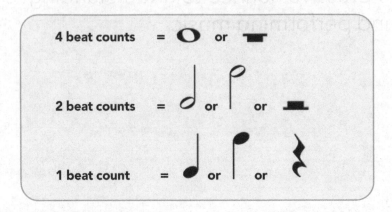

4 beat counts	=	○	or	▬	
2 beat counts	=	♩	or	♩	or ▬
1 beat count	=	♩	or	♩	or 𝄽

How to Write Whole, Half, and Quarter Rests

Whole Rests

1. Write a small, solid rectangle that "hangs" down from Line 4 of the staff.

2. The rectangle is the same length as a closed notehead.

3. The rest hangs down 50% of the way between Lines 4 and 3 of the staff.

4. In $\frac{4}{4}$, write whole rests at the beginning of measures on beat 1.

5. In $\frac{3}{4}$, write whole rests in the middle of the measure because it does not have 4 beats.

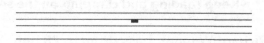

Half Rests

1. Write a small, solid rectangle that "rises" up from Line 3 of the staff.

2. The rectangle is the same length as a closed notehead.

3. The rest rises up 50% of the way between Lines 3 and 4.

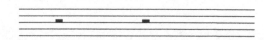

Quarter Rests

1. Write a diagonal line to the right, starting below Line 5 to Line 4 of the staff.

2. Write a diagonal line to the left, connecting Line 4 to Line 3.

3. Write a diagonal line to the right, ending before Line 2.

4. Write a line that curves to the left and down that ends before Line 1.

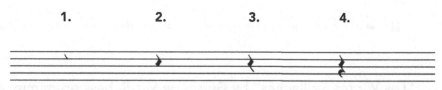

$\frac{4}{4}$ = whole rests at beginning of measures $\frac{3}{4}$ = whole rests in the middle of measures

Rests: Clap and Count

Clap Rests 1

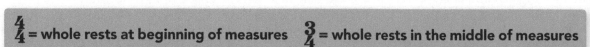

Clap Rests 2

60 19

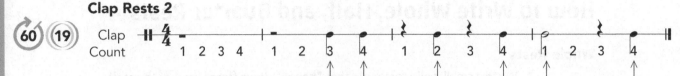

The next examples are from famous operas. Operas are performances of many pieces of music that together tell a story and are sung by opera singers. Operas are an example of when composers write words to their music. The instrument used in these examples is a bass drum, the ancestor of the kick drum. Bass drums are used in orchestral music and are written with the stem up. Clap and count!

> **Keep reading and clapping on the second line of music!**

"Rienzi" by Richard Wagner, bass drum p. 28 mm. 3–10 (Fürstner publication)

60 20

> **Measure numbers are used to show where in the piece of music the example is starting. In this example, 56 measures have already passed by.**

"Rusalka" by Antonín Dvořák, bass drum mm. 57–64

60 21

"Les Vêpres Siciliennes" by Giuseppe Verdi, bass drum mm. 45–55

60 22

How to Write Music 2

Measure Math 2

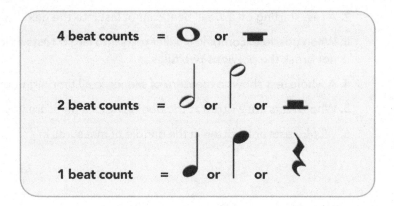

4 beat counts	= 𝅝 or 𝄻
2 beat counts	= 𝅗𝅥 or 𝅗𝅥 or 𝄼
1 beat count	= 𝅘𝅥 or 𝅘𝅥 or 𝄽

Measure Math 𝄴

Each measure in the incorrect example contains note and rest values that do not add up to 4. In the correct example, every measure contains note and rest values that add up to 4.

Incorrect

= 2 beats   = 6 beats   = 1 beat   = 3 beats

Correct

= 4 beats   ≈ 4 beats   = 4 beats   = 4 beats

Measure Math 𝄴

Each measure in the incorrect example contains note and rest values that do not add up to 3. In the correct example, every measure contains note and rest values that add up to 3.

Incorrect

= 1 beat = 4 beats   = 5 beats   = 2 beats

Correct

= 3 beats   = 3 beats   = 3 beats   = 3 beats

How to Write Notes and Rests in a Measure

Rest Rules

1. A rest starting on a strong beat can last into a weak beat.

2. A rest starting on a weak beat cannot last into the next beat(s). Use two separate rests.

3. When possible, combine smaller rests into larger rests as long as this does not break the previous two rules.

4. A whole rest shows a measure of silence in all time signatures.

5. Whole rests are written at the beginning of a measure in $\frac{4}{4}$.

6. Whole rests are written in the middle of measures in $\frac{3}{4}$.

Where to Write Notes and Rests 1

Memorize the order of strong and weak beats in $\frac{3}{4}$ and $\frac{4}{4}$ and on which beats all notes and rests can go.

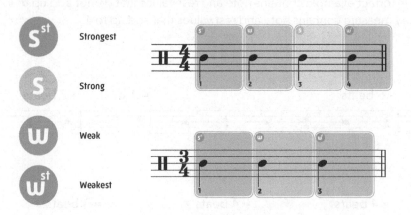

Sst	Strongest
S	Strong
w	Weak
wst	Weakest

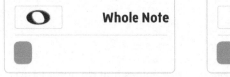 **Whole Note**

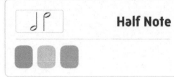 **Half Note**

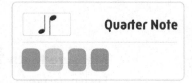 **Quarter Note**

 **Whole Rest**

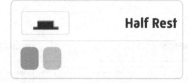 **Half Rest**

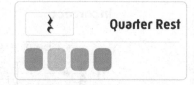 **Quarter Rest**

Explore these combinations and see correct and incorrect examples on the next page!

Examples in $\frac{4}{4}$

In $\frac{4}{4}$ there is an imaginary divide between beats 2 and 3 that only the whole note, whole rest, and half note can cross. To understand why the incorrect examples are wrong and the correct examples are right, see the rules and colors from the previous page.

Incorrect

Correct

Incorrect

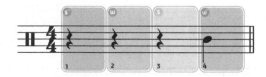

Correct

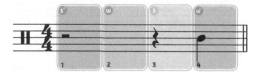

Incorrect

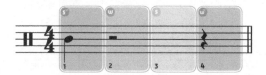

Correct

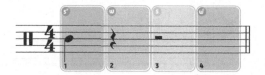

Dividing the Measure in Half $\frac{4}{4}$

To the right is a half note starting on beat 2. It **can** cross the "invisible divide." Neat!

Correct

Examples in $\frac{3}{4}$

Incorrect

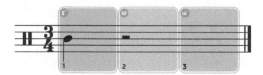

Correct

Incorrect

Correct

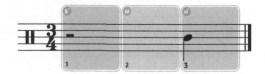

> When there is more than one line of staff, the plural is "staves"—not "staffs".

 # How to Write Lines of Music 2

How to Write Two Lines of Four Measures Each

1. Divide two staves into halves and quarters with bar lines.

2. Write a single bar line at the end (the right side) of the first line and a final bar line at the end (the right side) of the second line.

3. Write a percussion clef on both lines.

4. Write a time signature on the top line only.

5. Write notes and rests (not pictured).

1.

2.

3.

4.

Composition Ideas

These are a few ideas to get you started. There are many more combinations and permutations that can be made with a mix of whole, half, and quarter notes and rests. Perform your compositions to see how they sound and to make sure they line up with your intention and ideas. Create compositions around your feelings, ideas, thoughts, emotions, dreams, and experiences. Express anything and everything through music. Tell your story.

Two Consecutive Beats of Rest and Half Notes 4/4

One Beat of Rest and Half Notes 4/4

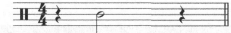

One Beat of Rest and Half Notes 3/4

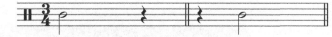

Two Consecutive Beats of Rest and Quarter Notes 4/4

Two Consecutive Beats of Rest and Quarter Notes 3/4

One Beat of Rest and Quarter Notes 4/4

One Beat of Rest and Quarter Notes 3/4

4/4 = whole rests at beginning of measures   3/4 = whole rests in middle of measures

Review: Rhythm 3

- Rests
  - Whole rests
  - Half rests
  - Quarter rests
- A whole rest can be used in any time signature to show a full measure of rest
- Measure Math 2
- How to write lines of music 2
- How to write notes and rests in a measure
- Where to write notes and rests
- Divide the measure in half in $\frac{4}{4}$
- Composition ideas

New Words You Should Know

1. Rests
2. Composition ideas

People who help others experience higher levels of fulfillment and live longer.

Would you help someone you've never met if it didn't cost you money, and you got credit for it?

If so, I have an "ask" to make on behalf of someone you do not know.

They are just like you were a few days, weeks, or years ago...less experienced, full of desire to get better at music, seeking information but unsure of where to look...this is where you come in.

Most people do judge a book by its cover (or at least its reviews). If you have found this book valuable so far, would you please take a brief moment right now and leave an honest review of the book and its contents? It will cost you zero dollars and less than 60 seconds.

Your review will help:
...one more person discover their calling in music.
...one more music student find the answers to their questions.
....one more life to change through the magic of music.

To make this happen...all you have to do is...
and this takes less than 60 seconds...leave a review.

Go to Amazon.com and search
The Best Music Theory Book for Beginners 1
Click on the book and scroll down to write a review, or scan this QR code to review.

Rhythm 4: Dots, Ties, and Repeat Signs

Dots unlock new note combinations, ties extend the duration of notes, and repeat signs save you valuable time and effort... read on to uncover the wonders of these musical elements!

Dotted Notes 1

Dotted notes are worth 1 ½ times the written note's rhythmic value.

Dotted Half Note

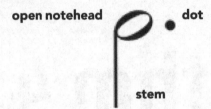

open notehead — dot

stem

The written note value + ½ of the written note value = dotted note value. Dotted half notes get three beat counts and can fill up an entire measure of $\frac{3}{4}$.

1   2   1   1   2   3

How to Write Dotted Notes

1. Write a note. In the example the note is a half note.

2. Write a small dot to the right of the notehead.

3. If the notehead is on a line, write the dot above the line the notehead is on.

4. If the notehead is in a space, write the dot in the same space as the notehead.

1.   **2.**   **3.**   **4.**

How to Write Dotted Notes in Measures

Dotted Half Note Rules

1. Just like with half notes, dotted half notes may cross the division between beats 2 and 3 in $\frac{4}{4}$.

2. Dotted half notes can start on the weak beat (beat 2) of $\frac{4}{4}$ only.

3. Dotted half notes fill up an entire measure of $\frac{3}{4}$.

Dotted Half Note

Correct

Correct

Dotted Notes: Clap and Count

> To hear how long the duration of a note is, you can say "taaaaaa" aloud on the attacks and hold the "ta" for the full count of the note.

Clap Dotted Notes 1

Clap Dotted Notes 2

Tied Notes

- Ties are curved lines that show notes are added together to make a single, long note.
- Only the first note gets an attack. Every note tied to the first note is not attacked.

Tie Math

Beat counts of first note + beat counts of second note = total beat counts of tied notes

Quarter Notes Tied To/From

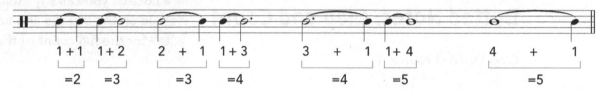

Half Notes Tied To/From

How to Write Tied Notes

Tied Notes on or above Line 3 of the Staff

1. Write the notes you wish to connect with a tie on the same line or space of the staff.

2. Write the tie from just above the first notehead to just above the second notehead.

1.   **2.**

Tied Notes below Line 3 of the Staff

1. Write the notes you wish to connect with a tie on the same line or space of the staff.

2. Write the tie from just below the first notehead to just below the second notehead.

1.   **2.**

How to Write Tied Notes in Measures

Tie Rules:

1. Only use ties when you cannot use a note that is worth the same number of beats.

2. Ties cannot skip over rests or other notes.

3. Ties on noteheads on or above Line 3 arch over, past the next line or space of the staff.

4. Ties on noteheads below Line 3 line arch under, past the next line or space of the staff..

5. Notes connected by ties must all be on the same line or space of the staff.

1. Incorrect

1. Correct

2. Incorrect

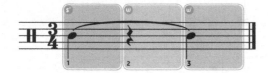

2. Correct

How to Write Tied Notes in Connecting Measures

1. Write the notes you wish to connect with a tie on the same line or space of the staff.

2. Write a tie showing that the notes are connected.

1.

2.

How to Write Tied Notes from One Line of Staff to the Next

1. Write the notes you wish to connect with a tie on the same staff line or space.

2. Show the beginning of the tie from the last note of the first line of staff (m. 4).

3. Show the end of the tie on the first note of the next line of staff (m. 5).

How to Tie More than Two Notes Together

1. Write the notes you wish to connect with a tie on the same line or space of the staff.

2. Write ties showing that the notes are connected.

3. There is no limit to the number of ties you can use in a row.

Tied Notes: Clap and Count

Clap Tied Notes 1

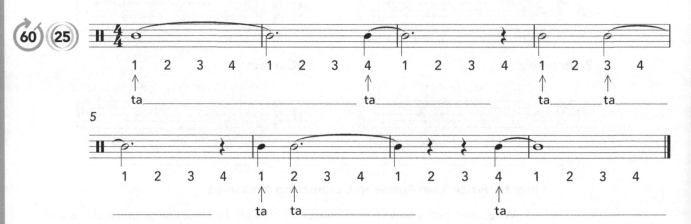

Clap Tied Notes 2

Repeat Signs

- Repeat signs are symbols that show a section of music should be played or sung again.

- Repeat signs mean you don't need to write the music twice.

Single Repeat Sign 1

1. Play/clap through the last measure.

2. Repeat back to measure 1.

3. Play/clap through to the last measure and stop.

Single Repeat Sign 2

This way of writing repeats works the same as the previous example (27). The only reason this way of writing repeats is in this book is because you may see it one day. When you want to write a single repeat sign, **do not use 2 repeat signs.** Write single repeats like in example (27).

1. Play/clap through the last measure.

2. Repeat back to measure 1.

3. Play/clap through to the last measure and stop.

Double Repeat Sign 1

1. Play/clap through the last measure.

2. Repeat back to the 𝄆 in measure 2. Do not play the first measure again.

3. Play/clap through the last measure and stop.

Double Repeat Sign 2

1. Play/clap up to the :‖ in measure 7.

2. Repeat back to the ‖: in measure 2. Do not play the first measure again.

3. Play/clap through the last measure and stop.

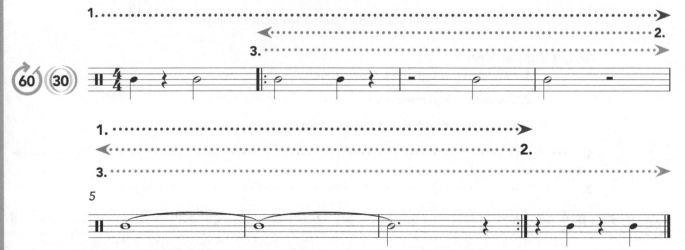

How to Write Repeat Signs

Start Repeat Sign

1. Write a backward final bar line.

2. Write a dot above and below Line 3 of the staff in Spaces 2 and 4.

End Repeat Sign

1. Write a final bar line.

2. Write a dot above and below Line 3 of the staff in Spaces 2 and 4.

How to Write Repeat Signs at the End of a Line of Staff

1. Prepare your staff with bar lines, a clef, a time signature, and a final bar line.

2. Write an end repeat sign by adding the dots in Spaces 2 and 4.

1.

2.

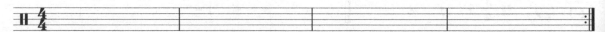

How to Write Repeat Signs in the Middle of a Line of Staff

1. Prepare your staff with bar lines, a clef, a time signature, and a final bar line.

2. Write a start repeat sign where you want the repeat to start.

3. Write an end repeat sign where you want the repeat to end.

1.

2.

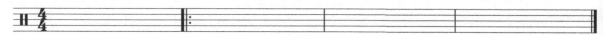

3.

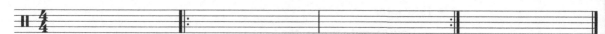

How to Write Repeat Signs Over Multiple Lines of Staff

1. Prepare your staff with bar lines, a clef, a time signature, and a final bar line.

2. Write a start repeat sign where you want the repeat to start and an end repeat sign where you want the repeat to end.

1.

2.

Review: Rhythm 4

- Dotted notes

    Dotted half note
    How to write dotted notes
    How to write dotted notes in measures

- Tied notes

    How to write tied notes
    Tie math
    How to write tied notes in measures
    How to write tied notes in connecting measures
    How to write tied notes from one line of staff to the next
    How to tie more than two notes together

- Repeat signs

    Single repeat sign 1
    Single repeat sign 2
    Double repeat sign 1
    Double repeat sign 2
    How to write repeat signs
    How to write repeat signs at the end of a line of staff
    How to write repeat signs in the middle of a line of staff

- How to write repeat signs over multiple lines of staff

Pitch and Notes 1: The Basics

This is a new musical world, where notes can sound low, high, and everywhere in between. You may now use digital music-writing software for your compositions!

High vs. Low Sounds

31

HIGH
PITCHES

32

LOW
PITCHES

A pitch is a single sound. Open your mouth and say "aaaah" just like you would at the doctor's or dentist's office. The sound you are making is a pitch. Some pitches are called notes. A note is a way of measuring certain pitches and giving those pitches names. More on that later!

Listen to and compare the high pitches and low pitches examples.

How Sound Is Made & Measured

Sound Waves

All sound is made up of waves. Vibration from striking the skin of a drum makes sound waves that travel through the air. Vibrations from plucking a guitar string travel as sound through the air. When sound waves reach the delicate membranes and bones in your ears, you hear sound.

Hertz

Hertz measure the speed of sound wave vibrations. Hertz are named after the German physicist Heinrich R. Hertz (1857–1894). "Hz" is the abbreviation for Hertz.

Sound Wave Cycles

A sound wave "cycles" as sound happens. The full cycle is when the sound wave curves up, down, and back to where it started.

One Cycle of a Sound Wave

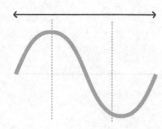

High Pitches

High pitches cycle faster, making more sound waves per second. They have larger "Hz" numbers.
880 Hz = 880 cycles per second = high pitch

Low Pitches

Low pitches cycle slower, making less sound waves per second. They have smaller "Hz" numbers.
55 Hz = 55 cycles per second = low pitch

You can hear all notes and see how many Hz they are by scanning the QR code.

High Pitches

- More sound waves (cycles) per second create higher pitches.
- Larger sound waves are louder.
- Smaller sound waves are quieter.

Large wave

Large wave = loud sound

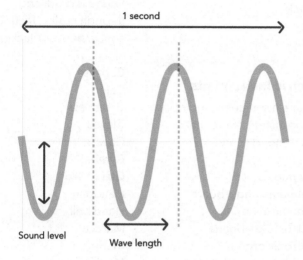

Small wave

Small wave = quiet sound

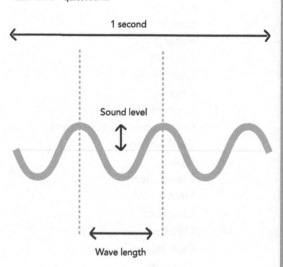

Low Pitches

- Fewer sound waves (cycles) per second create lower pitches.
- Larger sound waves are louder.
- Smaller sound waves are quieter.

Large wave

Large wave = loud sound

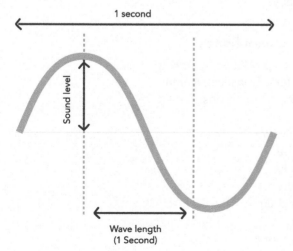

Small wave

Small wave = quiet sound

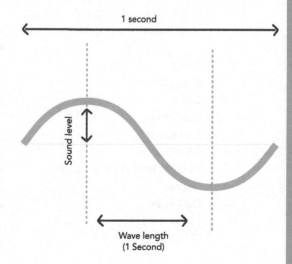

How Sound Is Made on Common Instruments

Aerophones

Sound is produced using air.

Accordion
Bagpipes
Bandoneon
Bassoon
Clarinet
Concertina
Cornet
Didgeridoo
Cor anglais (English horn)
Euphonium
Flute
French horn
Harmonica
Melodica
Oboe
Ocarina
Pan flute
Piccolo
Pipe organ
Recorder
Reed organ
Saxophone
Sousaphone
Trombone
Trumpet
Tuba
Whistle

Chordophones

Sound is produced by plucking or bowing the strings of the instrument.

Banjo
Bass guitar
Cello
Clavichord
Claviharp
Clavinet
Double bass (upright bass)
Guitar
Dulcimer
Harp
Harpsichord

Hurdy-gurdy
Lute
Lyre
Piano
Sitar
Ukulele
Viola
Violin

Electric Instruments

Require a source of electricity for the instrument to make the intended sound.

Bass pedals
Continuum fingerboard
Drum machine
Electronic keyboard
Electronic organ
Fingerboard synthesizer
Hammond organ
Jammer keyboard
Keyboard
Keytar
Laser harp
Mellotron
MIDI keyboard
Omnichord
Sampler
Synclavier
Synthesizer
Telharmonium
Theremin
Turntable

Membranophones

Sound is produced by striking a tightened plastic or animal membrane on the instrument.

Bass drum
Djembe
Drum kit
Kick drum
Snare drum
Tabla
Tambourine

Timpani
Tom drum

Idiophones

Sound is produced through rattles, friction, concussion, or plucking.

Cabassa
Cajón
Castanets
Claves
Cowbell
Cymbal
Glass harp
Handpan
Hand bell
Maraca
Marimba
Music box
Musical saw
Rattle
Singing bowl
Spoons
Steel drum
Triangle
Vibraphone
Washboard
Wood block
Xylophone

How Sound Is Defined

Tone

The word "tone" is used interchangeably with "pitch" to describe how high or low a sound is. Tone can also be used to describe "timbre."

Timbre

The quality of a sound.

- What makes a sound unique from other sounds.
- The "color" of a sound.

To understand timbre (pronounced tim-ber or tam-ber), compare the sound of three different instruments. Let's compare the violin, saxophone, and piano. They sound distinctly different because:

(33) **The Violin:**

- is a chordophone instrument (the performer makes sound unsing strings).
- has strings.
- is sounded with a horsehair bow (it can also be plucked by the performer's fingers).
- has a wooden body.

(34) **The Saxophone:**

- is an aerophone instrument (the performer makes sound using air).
- has a wood reed that vibrates.
- is sounded with the performer's breath.
- has a metal body.

(35) **The Piano:**

- is a chordophone instrument (the performer makes sound using strings).
- has strings.
- is sounded when the performer presses a key, which makes a hammer strike a string.
- has a metal and wooden body.

> These three instruments each have their own distinctive timbre, even when they play the same pitches in the same

Melody

A melody is a series of sequential pitches that take place over time. Many songwriters and composers try to make "pleasing" melodies. What you find pleasing may be different from what someone else finds pleasing. Melody is subjective, which means that everyone can feel differently about a melody, and no one is right or wrong — they have their opinions.

- Much of the time, pleasing melodies have some pattern that implies that the pitches belong together. This is a subjective statement, but your pattern-recognizing brain will find and enjoy the patterns of some melodies more than others.

- You will learn how to write full melodies in *The Best Music Theory Book for Beginners 3*. For now, focus on enjoying and remembering the way the music sounds.

(36)

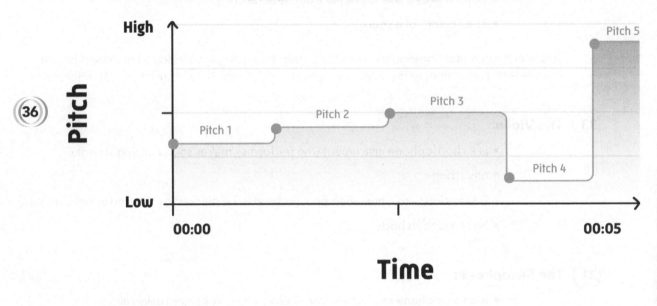

(37) **Melody Example 1**

(38) **Melody Example 2**

Notes

Notes are names that we give to certain pitches. The story behind why only some pitches get names is long and complicated, involves ancient China and Greece, and includes a bunch of math. For now, here are the facts to know.

> **Note Rules:**
>
> **1.** Notes are written and spoken with letters from the alphabet.
>
> **2.** Notes are pitches. These pitches get letter names.
>
> **3.** We give different letters to different pitches.
>
> **4.** There is a pattern to how we assign the letters.
>
> **5.** The letter pattern repeats over and over again.

The Basic Musical Alphabet:

A B C D E F G

- The first seven letters of the regular English alphabet.
- Repeats back to A after G.
- These letters are note names, which is a way of giving names to pitches.
- Ascends infinitely.
- Descends infinitely.
- Begin on any of the seven letters and count up or down the basic musical alphabet in ascending or descending order.

The Basic Musical Alphabet: Circle

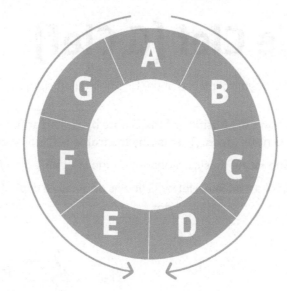

(39) Count down the musical alphabet (notes go lower)

Count up the musical alphabet (notes go higher)

The Basic Musical Alphabet: Vertical

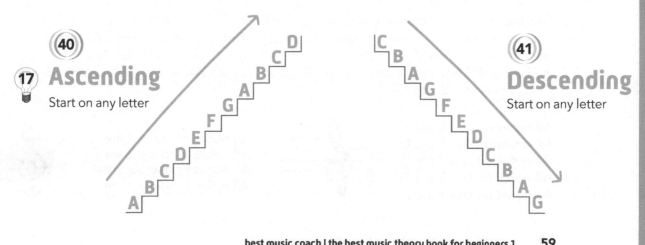

(40) (17) **Ascending**
Start on any letter

(41) **Descending**
Start on any letter

Notes on the Staff

Reminder: Staff (one), staves (plural): a group of five horizontal lines.

> - Notes are placed on the lines and in the spaces of the staff to show different pitches.
> - Higher sounding notes are toward the top of the staff (up toward the ceiling).
> - Lower sounding notes are toward the bottom of the staff (down toward the floor).

1. Line notes: lowest to highest sounding
2. Line notes: highest to lowest sounding
3. Space notes: lowest to highest sounding
4. Space notes: highest to lowest sounding

High notes

Low notes

Treble Clef (G Clef)

The treble clef is a symbol placed at the beginning (left side) of a line of staff.

> - Shows the position of the G note by curling around Line 2 of the staff, where the "G note" goes. (That is why the treble clef is also called the "G clef".)
> - Shows the musical alphabet on the staff based on the position of the G note.
> - Looks a bit like a letter G (it was originally a capital G when it was invented).

G line ‑‑‑> **Treble clef**

How to Read Notes on the Staff

Each line and space of the staff gives any note that lands on or in it a letter name. Any note on Line 5 is always "F." Any note in Space 1 is always called "F." These are two different F notes (more on that later). Any note on Line 1 is "E." Any note on Line 2 is "G." Any note on Line 3 is "B." Any note on Line 4 is "D." Any note in Space 2 is "A." Any note in Space 3 is "C." Any note in Space 4 is "E."

All notes on line 5 are F
All notes on line 4 are D
All notes on line 3 are B
All notes on line 2 are G
All notes on line 1 are E

All notes in space 4 are E
All notes in space 3 are C
All notes in space 2 are A
All notes in space 1 are F

How to Remember the Notes on the Staff

The note on Line 1 of the staff is E. The musical alphabet starts on E (Line 1), goes in order through E again (Space 4), finishing on F (Line 5). Memorize the notes with the mnemonic and FACE tricks below.

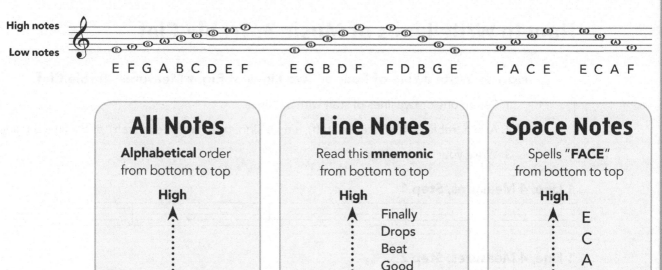

E F G A B C D E F   E G B D F   F D B G E   F A C E   E C A F

All Notes
Alphabetical order from bottom to top

High
↑
Low

Line Notes
Read this **mnemonic** from bottom to top

High
↑
Finally
Drops
Beat
Good
Every
Low

Space Notes
Spells **"FACE"** from bottom to top

High
↑
E
C
A
F
Low

18 How to Write a Treble Clef

1 Write a curved line from Line 2 to Line 3, then back down to Line 2.
2 Write a curved line from Line 2 to Line 1, then up to Line 3.
3 Write a tilted backward letter "S" from Line 3 to above the staff.
4 Write a line down through the clef to below the staff with a curl back to the left and up.

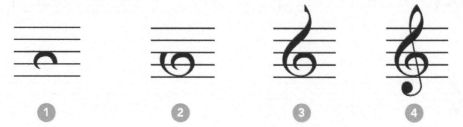

1   2   3   4

You can now write compositions and exercises using a treble clef in the place of a percussion clef. If you play an instrument or can sight sing, play your compositions! You can use digital music software like Noteflight, Sibelius, or Finale to write and hear your compositions without playing or needing an instrument!

19 How to Write Music 3: Treble Clef

How to Write Lines of Music 3: Treble Clef

How to Write a Line of Four or Two Lines of Eight Measures: Treble Clef

1. Set up one or two lines of staff with bar lines.

2. Add a treble clef (all lines of staff), a time signature (first line of staff), and a final bar line.

3. Write your composition.

1 Line, 4 Measures, Step 1

1 Line, 4 Measures, Step 2

1 Line, 4 Measures, Step 3

2 Lines, 8 Measures, Step 2

2 Lines, 8 Measures, Step 3

Ledger Lines

- Short horizontal lines above or below the staff.

- Extend the ascending and descending musical alphabet away from the staff.

- Used for writing notes that are higher or lower than the notes on the staff.

- FACE pattern repeats on ledger lines above the staff starting on Line 5 (without the E). FACE patten repeats from ledger line 3 below the staff up to Line 1 of the staff.

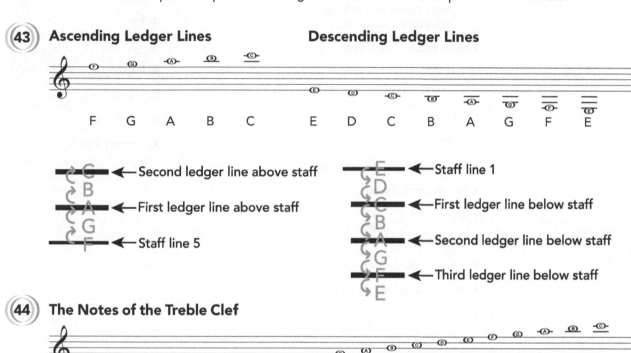

(43) Ascending Ledger Lines   Descending Ledger Lines

F   G   A   B   C   E   D   C   B   A   G   F   E

Second ledger line above staff ← ... → Staff line 1

First ledger line above staff ← ... → First ledger line below staff

Staff line 5 ← ... → Second ledger line below staff

Third ledger line below staff

(44) The Notes of the Treble Clef

E F G A B C D E F G A B C D E F G A B C

How to Write Notes on Ledger Lines

Ledger Line Rules:

1. Ledger lines are thicker than the lines of the staff.

2. Ledger lines extend on either side of the notehead.

3. Ledger lines do not touch other ledger lines and there is the same vertical space between ledger lines as there is between staff lines.

4. The stem of notes on or below one ledger line is 4 staff lines long, just like other notes.

5. The stem of noteheads past one ledger line above or below the staff extend to Line 3.

6. Dotted notes and tied notes work the same way with ledger lines.

1., 2.   **3.**   **4.**   **5.**

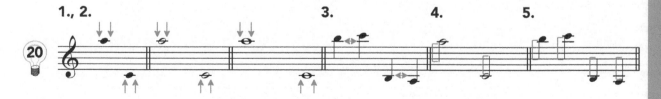

Review: Pitch and Notes 1

- High vs. low sounds
- How sound is made and measured
    - Sound waves
    - Hertz
    - How sound is made on common instruments
- How sound is defined
    - Tone
    - Timbre
- Melody
- Notes
- The basic musical alphabet
- Notes on the staff
- Treble clef
- How to read notes on the staff
- How to remember notes on the staff
- How to write a treble clef
- Ledger lines

New Words You Should Know

1. Pitch
2. Tone
3. Timbre
4. Melody
5. Notes
6. Treble clef
7. Ledger line

Name the Notes

Write the note letter underneath each note:

Answer Key:

F, G, A, B, C, C, B, B, A, A, G, G, F, F, A, C

E, G, F, A, C, B, E, D, E, C, D, B, D, E, F, G

Pitch and Notes 2: Theory

Jump in and see what happens when we look a little deeper into the "how" and "why" of pitch and notes!

Get to Know the Piano

Even if you do not plan on playing the piano, understanding the way it works is helpful for music theory, since you can see the notes and the distances between the notes on the piano keyboard.

(45) The 12-Key Pattern

12-Key Pattern Breakdown - Part 1

There is a pattern that repeats every 12 keys on the piano.

Part 1 of the pattern is three white keys (1, 3, 5) that are around the two black keys (2, 4).
3 white + 2 black = 5 keys. The white key all the way to the left (key 1) is first in the 12-key pattern.

12 Keys - Part 1

12-Key Pattern Breakdown - Part 2

Part 2 of the pattern is four white keys (6, 8, 10, 12) that are around the three black keys (7, 9, 11).
4 white + 3 black = 7 keys. The white key all the way to the right (key 12) is last in the 12-key pattern.

12 Keys - Part 2

The Complete 12-Key Pattern

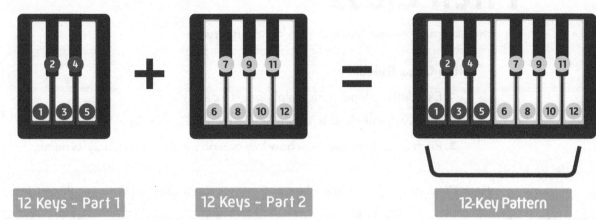

12 Keys - Part 1 + 12 Keys - Part 2 = 12-Key Pattern

How the Full 12-Key Pattern Repeats

The 12-key pattern repeats over and over again for the entire keyboard. Every time it repeats, it sounds higher than the last 12-key group when going from left to right.

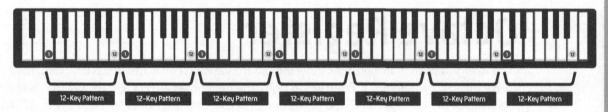

12-Key Pattern   12-Key Pattern   12-Key Pattern   12-Key Pattern   12-Key Pattern   12-Key Pattern   12-Key Pattern

(46) The Basic Musical Alphabet: White Keys

- Start on the letter C of the basic musical alphabet.

- C is the name of the first key in the 12-key pattern.

- It is called the C key because when you press it, the piano makes a C note.

12 Keys - Part 1 + 12 Keys - Part 2 = 12-Key Pattern

The Basic Musical Alphabet on the Keyboard

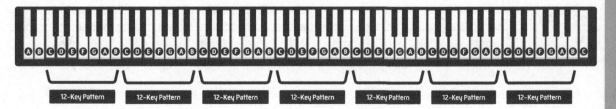

12-Key Pattern   12-Key Pattern   12-Key Pattern   12-Key Pattern   12-Key Pattern   12-Key Pattern   12-Key Pattern

Pitch Class

A pitch class is all the notes that share the same letter name.

Pitch Class Rules:

1. Each letter of the musical alphabet is a pitch class.

2. All As are a pitch class, as are Bs, Cs, Ds, Es, Fs, and Gs.

3. Pitch class does not show how low or high a note sounds, only its name.

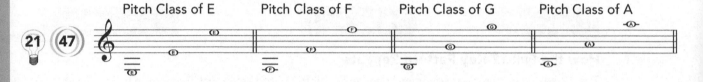

Octave Register

Octave registers are numbers that show the difference between notes in a pitch class. The lowest C on a piano keyboard is C1. From left to right, the next notes are D1, E1, F1, G1, A1, and B1. The register number changes on C; the note after B1 is C2. The next notes are D2, E2, F2, G2, A2, and B2. The next note is C3. This pattern continues until the highest C; C8. Notes below C1 are written with 0. The note to the left of C1 is B0.

Octave Registers on the Staff

E3 F3 G3 A3 B3 C4 D4 E4 F4 G4 A4 B4 C5 D5 E5 F5 G5 A5 B5 C6

Octave Registers: Hear the Difference

Hear different octave registers of the same pitch class for E, F, G, and A.

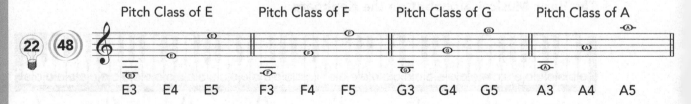

E3   E4   E5   F3   F4   F5   G3   G4   G5   A3   A4   A5

⑭ Octaves

Octaves on a Piano Keyboard

An octave (oct = 8 like octopus or octagon) is the eight notes between each octave register of each pitch class. There are 8 notes between C4 (middle C) and C5. That distance of 8 notes is an octave. From high to low, C5 to C4 is also an octave. The same idea applies to any note. D3 up to D4 is an octave, D4 down to D3 is an octave. F4 up to F5 is an octave, just like F5 down to F4 is an octave.

> **pitch class + same pitch class 1 octave register higher or lower = octave**

From C to C is an octave

From Any A to A is an octave

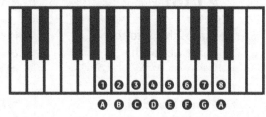

From Any E to E is an octave

From Any D to D is an octave

Octaves on the Staff: Treble Clef

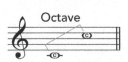
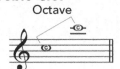
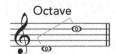
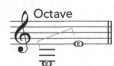

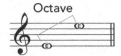
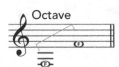
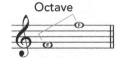
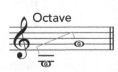

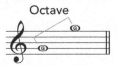
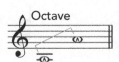
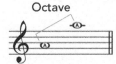
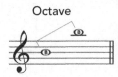

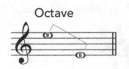
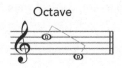

Accidentals 1

- A musical symbol that raises or lowers a note's pitch or returns a changed note to its original pitch.

- In addition to the symbol, the note that is raised, lowered, or returned to its original pitch can also be called an accidental.

- You will see accidentals in several forms in this and other Best Music Coach books to prepare you for seeing accidentals in different fonts and handwritings in the real world!

♭ **Flat**	♮ **Natural**	# **Sharp**
Makes the note sound at a lower pitch.	Returns a sharp (raised) or flat (lowered) note to its original pitch.	Makes the note sound at a higher pitch.
"Flat" is added to the note name.	**"Natural" is added to the note name.**	**"Sharp" is added to the note name.**
Say: "D flat."	**Say:** "D natural."	**Say:** "D sharp."

D5   D♭5   D5

D5   D#5   D5

23 How to Write Accidentals

Flat

1. Write a vertical line.

2. Write another line: curved on top and straight at the bottom.

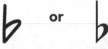

Natural

1. Write an uppercase "L."

2. Write an upside-down uppercase L connected to the first L.

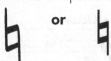

Sharp

1. Write two parallel, vertical lines.

2. Write two shorter, parallel horizontal lines. Think "hashtag."

        or

How to Write Accidentals in Front of Notes

Accidentals are written in front (to the left) of the notehead—never behind it. Because the accidental changes the note, anyone reading the music needs to know about the change to the note before they read or play it, not after.

1. Place the accidental to the left of the notehead, as close to the notehead as you can without touching the notehead.

2. **Accidentals in a Space**
   Fill the space with the hole in the middle of the accidental.

3. **Accidentals on a Line**
   Align the hole in the middle of the accidental on the line.

Author's note:

The "hole" of the accidental is not technically a music theory term, but what else are we going to call it? "The empty void betwixt the lines of the accidental"? See what I mean? No good way of describing that thing.

How to Write Accidentals in a Measure

1. Notes are natural unless they have an accidental. Don't write ♮ for all natural notes.

2. Accidentals change the note they are in front of for one measure only.

3. Accidentals change notes of one pitch class and octave register for one measure.
   Same pitch class + different octave register = no change

4. Natural accidentals cancel sharp or flat accidentals in the measure they are written.

5. Accidentals that are tied to another measure or line change all notes in the tied group.

Courtesy Accidentals

How Do Courtesy Accidentals Work?

Courtesy accidentals are extra accidentals to remind the performer which note to play. Courtesy accidentals are a way to be nice to anyone who is playing your music. It makes their job much easier and clearer, which will usually result in a better performance!

Example 1

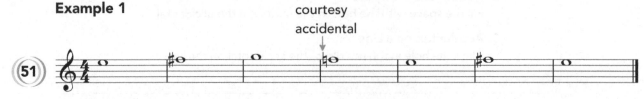

Example 1: What Makes This a Courtesy Accidental?

In measure 4 there is a courtesy accidental. It does not need to be there. The ♯ accidental in measure 2 only changes the F to an F♯ for that measure. The next time the performer sees an F note of the same octave register (same line of the staff), they are kindly reminded to play an F♮.

Example 2

Example 2: What Makes This a Courtesy Accidental?

In measure 2 there is a courtesy accidental. It does not need to be there. The ♯ accidental on beat 4 of measure 1 carries over to beat 1 of measure 2 because of the tie. Once the tied notes are completed, the accidental has no more power. The next time the performer sees an F note of the same register on beat 2, they are kindly reminded to play an F♮. In measure 3, there are two courtesy accidentals. These are here to remind you that only the F on Line 5 has the ♯ accidental. All other octave registers of the pitch class F are not changed by the accidental.

Example 3: Accidentals Tied to Another Line of Staff

When accidentals are tied to another line, it is nice to write a courtesy accidental in parentheses.

> ### How to Write Courtesy Accidentals in a Measure
>
> 1. Write courtesy accidentals in any measure where it will make the notes more obvious for the reader/performer.
>
> 2. Write courtesy accidentals on other octave registers of the pitch class that have the accidental.

Enharmonic Equivalents

A pitch that has two different note names is an enharmonic equivalent. To be clear, **one** pitch has **two** note names. Both note names are "spelled" (written) differently, but the pitch sounds the same for both. Enharmonics are like the words **to**, **too**, and **two** that sound the same when you say them, but have different meanings when you write them.

Enharmonic equivalents = same sound with two different names

Notes are "spelled" by writing the note and any needed accidentals.

(53)

C♯ D♭	D♯ E♭	E F♭	E♯ F	F♯ G♭	G♯ A♭	A♯ B♭	B C♭	B♯ C
Same Sound	Same Sound	Same Sound	Same Sound	Same Sound	Same Sound	Same Sound	Same Sound	Same Sound

The Full Musical Alphabet:
The 12 Notes of Music

The complete musical alphabet. These are the 12 notes used in "classical," CCM, hard rock, metal, pop, rock, blues, and jazz.

All the songs in all these genres use the same 12 notes!

The less common enharmonic equivalents are in parentheses. They are rarely used.

 25 (54) **Count down the musical alphabet**

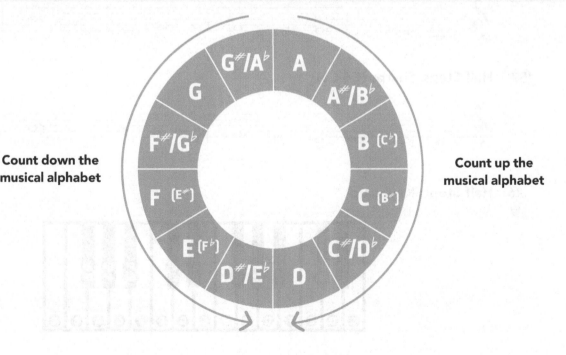

Count up the musical alphabet

Half Step (Semitone)

A half step is the smallest distance between two notes. Another way of saying half step is "semitone."

> • The distance of one half-step (semitone) is from the starting note to its neighbor, either lower (to the left) or higher (to the right) in the full musical alphabet.
>
> • There are 12 half steps in an octave.

∧ = One Half-Step

(55) Half Steps: The Full Musical Alphabet

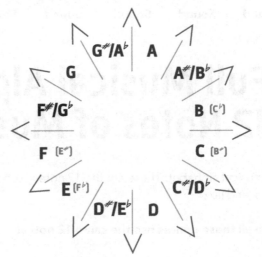

(56) Half Steps: Flats (C4-C5)

(57) Half Steps: Sharps (C4-C5)

(26) Half Steps: Keyboard

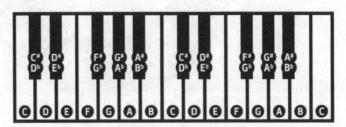

Whole Step (Whole Tone)

The distance of one whole-step (whole tone) is equal to two half steps (semitones).

- There are two groups of whole-steps with six notes each.
- Beginning on A, there are six notes (Whole Steps 1).
- Beginning on A♯/B♭ there are six different notes (Whole Steps 2).
- Begin on any note of the musical alphabet.

 = One Whole Step

58 **Whole Steps 1: The Musical Alphabet**

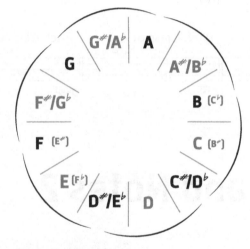

59 **Whole Steps 2: The Musical Alphabet**

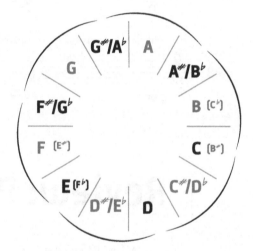

Whole Steps: Flats

60 **Whole Steps 1**

Whole Steps 2

Whole Steps: Sharps

61 **Whole Steps 1**

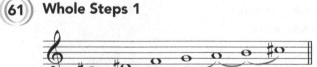

Whole Steps 2

27 **Whole Steps 1: Keyboard**

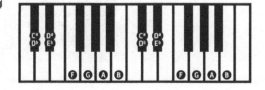

Whole Steps 2: Keyboard

Pitch Class 2: Accidentals

A pitch class is all notes that share the same letter name and accidental.

Pitch Class with Accidentals Rules:

1. Each letter of the musical alphabet is a pitch class.

2. All As are a pitch class, as are Bs, Cs, Ds, Es, Fs, and Gs.

3. A letter name with an accidental is a different pitch class. G notes are a different pitch class than all G♯ notes. All G♭ notes are another pitch class.

4. Pitch class does not show how low or high a note sounds, only its name.

Review: Pitch and Notes 2

- The 12-key pattern
- The basic musical alphabet on the keyboard
- Pitch class
- Octave register
- Octaves
- Accidentals
- How to write accidentals

    How to write accidentals in front of notes
    How to write accidentals in a measure

- Courtesy accidentals

    How to write courtesy accidentals in a measure

- Enharmonic equivalents
- The full musical alphabet: the 12 notes of music
- Half step
- Whole step

New Words You Should Know

1. Pitch class
2. Octave register
3. Octave
4. Accidentals
5. Flat
6. Natural
7. Sharp
8. Courtesy accidentals
9. Enharmonic
10. Half step
11. Whole step

Pitch and Notes 3: Scales

Scales are a framework for organizing and analyzing notes...and because every part of music has notes, scales are ridiculously useful.

What Are Scales?

Scales are a collection of notes in musical alphabetical order from lowest to highest sounding or from highest to lowest sounding.

> **Scale Rules:**
>
> 1. A scale from lowest note to highest is called an ascending scale and a scale from highest note to lowest is a descending scale.
>
> 2. Scales begin and end on the same pitch class one octave apart.
>
> 3. The name of the scale is the pitch class it starts on, followed by the type of scale.

Chromatic Scale

12-Note Scale (Dodecatonic)

The name "chromatic" comes from the word "chroma" which means "color" in Greek. With this scale you hear all 12 notes in the octave (all 12 musical "colors"), making it a very colorful scale!

> **Chromatic Scale Rules:**
>
> 1. Use all 12 notes of the musical alphabet with the correct enharmonic equivalents.
>
> 2. If you start the scale with flats, use only flat and natural accidentals. Do not add sharps.
>
> 3. If you start the scale with sharps, use only sharp and natural accidentals. Do not use flats.
>
> 4. Can begin on any note of the musical alphabet.

A few chromatic notes (half steps) in a row is called a chromaticism.

⌢ = One Half-Step

62 **C Chromatic Scale: Flats**

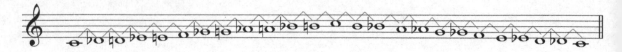

63 **C Chromatic Scale: Sharps**

How to Write Chromatic Scales

1. Write a treble clef and a double bar line on a single line of staff.

2. Ascending: Begin on C4, C5, G3, or G4.

3. Descending: Begin on C6, C5, G5, or G4.

4. Start and end on the same pitch class.

5. Write all 12 notes and the starting pitch class one octave higher or lower.

6. Use the full musical alphabet for guidance so you write the correct enharmonic equivalents. Use common enharmonic spellings. Use C, not B#.

7. Write the scale name above the staff.

How to Write a Chromatic Scale with Flats

1. Only use natural and flat notes to write all 12 notes.

Ascending

C Chromatic Scale

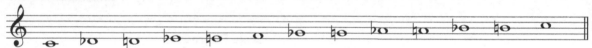

Descending

C Chromatic Scale

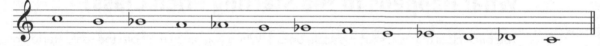

How to Write a Chromatic Scale with Sharps

1. Only use natural and sharp notes to write all 12 notes.

Ascending

C Chromatic Scale

Descending

C Chromatic Scale

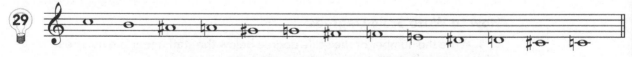

Memorize the full musical alphabet.

Scale Degrees

Scale degrees are a specific name and/or number given to a note of an ascending scale. Scale degrees are used to identify notes in scales. Scale degree numbers stay the same for any octave register.

Why Do We Use Scale Degrees?

1. To help us tell the difference between scale degrees and other music theory systems that use numbers.

2. To know which note of the scale we are talking about.

How to Identify Scale Degrees

Each scale degree has a caret or "roof" above it. If the first note of a scale is C, then we say that C is scale degree $\hat{1}$.

> Scale degrees are assigned to notes based on the ascending scale.
> In the C Chromatic Scale, B♮ is the 12th scale degree, even if you
> are writing a descending scale.

Scale Degrees											
$\hat{1}$	$\hat{2}$	$\hat{3}$	$\hat{4}$	$\hat{5}$	$\hat{6}$	$\hat{7}$	$\hat{8}$	$\hat{9}$	$\hat{10}$	$\hat{11}$	$\hat{12}$

What Happens to the Starting Pitch Class?

The pitch class that you start the scale on is $\hat{1}$. When you reach the note the scale started on one octave higher, label it as $\hat{1}$ again or as $\hat{1}$ with a $(\hat{13})$ or $(\hat{8})$ (learn about the 8 on the next page) in brackets to show that the note is the same pitch class as the starting note one octave higher.

Ascending Scale Degrees

Descending Scale Degrees

> ### How to Write Scale Degrees
> **1.** Write the number of the scale degree below the staff under the notehead.
>
> **2.** Write the "roof" or caret above the number.

Diatonic Major Scales 1

7-Note Scale (Heptatonic)

Diatonic means anything to do with the major scale. The word comes from ancient Greek, and literally means "major scale." You can call this scale the "major scale" without the word "diatonic."

> **Major Scale Rules:**
>
> **1.** All major scales can be understood, written, and performed with a formula of whole and half steps (Whole, Whole, Half, Whole, Whole, Whole, Half).
>
> **2.** Begins and ends on the same pitch class, one octave apart.
>
> **3.** Major scales can start on any note of the full musical alphabet.
>
> **4.** One of each letter is used (one A, B, C, D, E, F, and G) before the pitch class that the scale started on repeats. There is "some kind of" A, B, C, D, E, F, and G in every major scale. F and F♯ are never in the same major scale.
>
> **5.** Either sharps or flats are used in a major scale. Major scales never have both sharp and flat accidentals.
>
> **6.** The Major Step Formula stays the same for all major scales.
>
> **7.** The first whole step happens between $\hat{1}$ and $\hat{2}$.

(64) C Major Scale

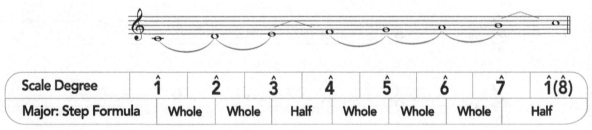

Scale Degree	$\hat{1}$	$\hat{2}$	$\hat{3}$	$\hat{4}$	$\hat{5}$	$\hat{6}$	$\hat{7}$	$\hat{1}(\hat{8})$
Major: Step Formula	Whole	Whole	Half	Whole	Whole	Whole	Half	

(65) G Major Scale

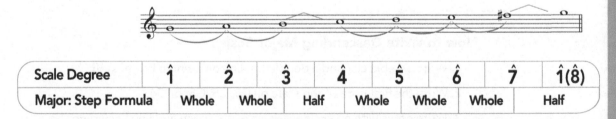

Scale Degree	$\hat{1}$	$\hat{2}$	$\hat{3}$	$\hat{4}$	$\hat{5}$	$\hat{6}$	$\hat{7}$	$\hat{1}(\hat{8})$
Major: Step Formula	Whole	Whole	Half	Whole	Whole	Whole	Half	

(30) Major Scales: Rules and Accidentals in the G Major Scale (Example (65))

Rule 4: $\hat{7}$ is not G♭. There was already "some kind of" G on $\hat{1}$. The only letter remaining is F.
Rule 6: To keep the formula of whole and half steps, $\hat{7}$ is raised an extra half-step with a sharp accidental. If it was left as F♮ that would not work with the formula since E to F♮ is one half-step and we need a whole step between scale degrees $\hat{6}$ and $\hat{7}$.

How to Write Major Scales

How to Write Ascending Major Scales

1. Write a treble clef and a double bar line on a single line of staff.

2. Write the first note of the scale on C4, C5, G3, or G4.
(We will get to the other keys in the next books.)

3. Write notes with no accidentals on every space and line, including the
pitch class one octave higher than the note you started on.

4. Write the Major Step Formula, using the curved lines for whole
steps below the notes and angled lines (a roof or caret) for half steps (optional).

5. Add in the accidentals needed to make each note the correct distance
from the last according to the Major Step Formula.

Ascending Major Scales

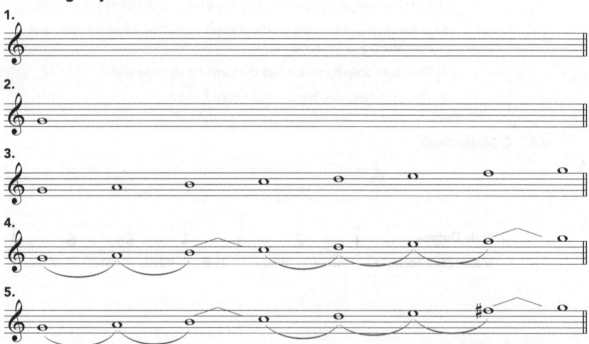

How to Write Descending Major Scales

1. Write a treble clef and a double bar line on a single line of staff.

2. Write the first note of the scale on C6, C5, G5, or G4.

3. Write notes with no accidentals on every space and line, including the
pitch class one octave lower than the note you started on.

4. Write the Major Step Formula, using the curved lines for whole
steps below the notes and angled lines (a roof or caret) for half steps (optional).

5. Add in the accidentals needed to make each note the correct distance
from the last according to the Major Step Formula.

Descending Major Scales

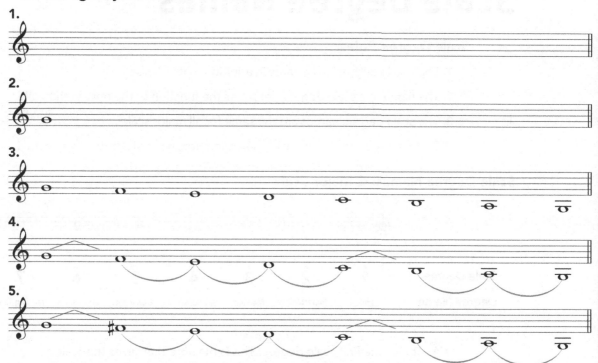

How to Write Ascending + Descending Major Scales

1. Write a treble clef and a double bar line on a single line of staff and the first note of the scale on C4, C5, G3, or G4.

2. Write notes with no accidentals on every space and line, including the pitch class one octave higher than the note you started on, and on every space and line back down to the note you started on.

3. Write the whole- and half-step formula, using the curved lines for whole steps below the notes and angled lines for half steps (optional).

4. Add in the accidentals needed to make each note the correct distance from the last according to the Major Step Formula. You can include an extra "very courteous" courtesy accidental for the descending part of the scale for clarity, but this is optional.

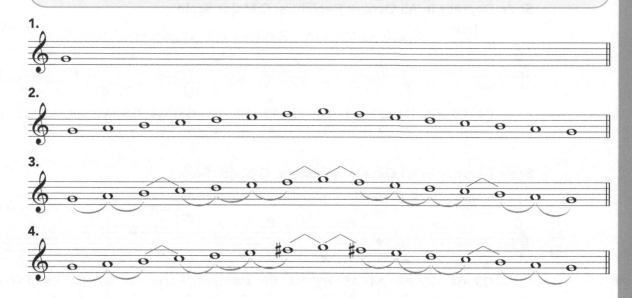

Scale Degree Names

Scale Degree Rules:

1. Each scale degree has a name in addition to its number.

2. The name of a scale degree describes the function of the note in the scale.

3. The scale degree names are the same for all major scales.

4. Scale degrees names apply to the entire pitch class of a note in **any** octave register.

Scale Degree Names: C Major Scale

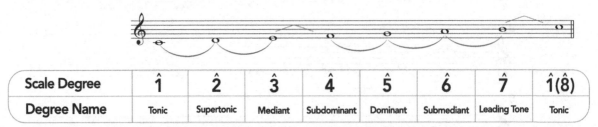

Scale Degree	$\hat{1}$	$\hat{2}$	$\hat{3}$	$\hat{4}$	$\hat{5}$	$\hat{6}$	$\hat{7}$	$\hat{1}(\hat{8})$
Degree Name	Tonic	Supertonic	Mediant	Subdominant	Dominant	Submediant	Leading Tone	Tonic

- $\hat{1}$ - **Tonic** - the first scale degree. This is the note that gives the scale its name. If the Tonic is a C, the scale is a "C" major scale. $\hat{8}$ is also the tonic.

- $\hat{2}$ - **Supertonic** - super means above. The note **above** the Tonic.

- $\hat{3}$ - **Mediant** - think: the median that divides the traffic on a highway. The third degree of the scale divides the notes between the Tonic $\hat{1}$ and Dominant $\hat{5}$.

- $\hat{4}$ - **Subdominant** - "sub" means "below" (think: submarine). The Subdominant is one note below the Dominant.

- $\hat{5}$ - **Dominant** - the second-most important note after the Tonic.

- $\hat{6}$ - **Submediant** - is between the Dominant and the octave of the Tonic.

- $\hat{7}$ - **Leading Tone** - also called a "tendency tone," the Leading Tone "leads" the scale back home to the octave of the Tonic.

Scale Degrees in All Octave Registers: C Major Scale

C4	C5	C6	D4	D5	E3	E4	E5	F3	F4	F5	G3	G4	G5	A3	A4	A5	B3	B4	B5
$\hat{1}$	$\hat{1}$	$\hat{1}$	$\hat{2}$	$\hat{2}$	$\hat{3}$	$\hat{3}$	$\hat{3}$	$\hat{4}$	$\hat{4}$	$\hat{4}$	$\hat{5}$	$\hat{5}$	$\hat{5}$	$\hat{6}$	$\hat{6}$	$\hat{6}$	$\hat{7}$	$\hat{7}$	$\hat{7}$

Scale Degrees in All Octave Registers: G Major Scale

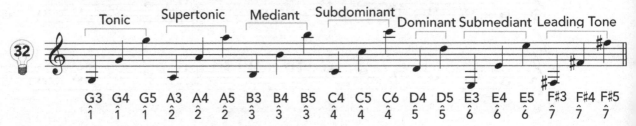

G3	G4	G5	A3	A4	A5	B3	B4	B5	C4	C5	C6	D4	D5	E3	E4	E5	F#3	F#4	F#5
$\hat{1}$	$\hat{1}$	$\hat{1}$	$\hat{2}$	$\hat{2}$	$\hat{2}$	$\hat{3}$	$\hat{3}$	$\hat{3}$	$\hat{4}$	$\hat{4}$	$\hat{4}$	$\hat{5}$	$\hat{5}$	$\hat{6}$	$\hat{6}$	$\hat{6}$	$\hat{7}$	$\hat{7}$	$\hat{7}$

(66) Tetrachords

"Tetra" means four. Tetrachords are a group of any four notes. This is the original way the ancient Greeks who invented the diatonic major scale thought about major scales.

> **Tetrachord Rules:**
>
> **1.** Each tetrachord has a formula of Whole, Whole, Half.
>
> **2.** All major scales have two tetrachords.
>
> **3.** The two tetrachords are connected by one whole-step.

Tetrachord 1

The first tetrachord begins on the Tonic.

C Major Tetrachord

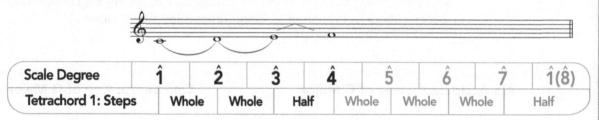

Scale Degree	$\hat{1}$	$\hat{2}$	$\hat{3}$	$\hat{4}$	$\hat{5}$	$\hat{6}$	$\hat{7}$	$\hat{1}(\hat{8})$
Tetrachord 1: Steps	Whole	Whole	Half	Whole	Whole	Whole	Half

Tetrachord 2

The second tetrachord begins on the dominant ($\hat{5}$). All major scales start with Whole, Whole, Half. The second tetrachord is the first 4 notes of a G major scale! Imagine $\hat{5}$ is $\hat{1}$.

G Major Tetrachord

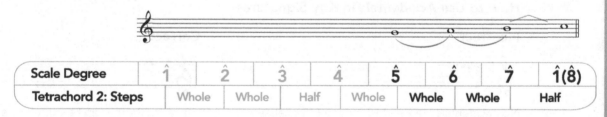

Scale Degree	$\hat{1}$	$\hat{2}$	$\hat{3}$	$\hat{4}$	$\hat{5}$	$\hat{6}$	$\hat{7}$	$\hat{1}(\hat{8})$
Tetrachord 2: Steps	Whole	Whole	Half	Whole	Whole	Whole	Half

(33) Tetrachord 1 + Tetrachord 2 = Major Scale

C Major Tetrachord + Whole Step + G Major Tetrachord = C Major Scale

The extra whole-step is between $\hat{4}$ and $\hat{5}$.

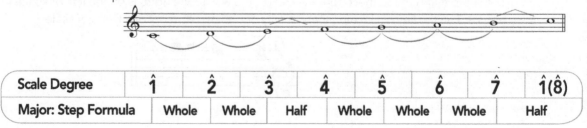

Scale Degree	$\hat{1}$	$\hat{2}$	$\hat{3}$	$\hat{4}$	$\hat{5}$	$\hat{6}$	$\hat{7}$	$\hat{1}(\hat{8})$
Major: Step Formula	Whole	Whole	Half	Whole	Whole	Whole	Half

Key Signatures 1

Every major scale is related to a key. A key is all the notes of a scale. The key of C is all the notes of a C major scale. When you write or perform music with a key signature you are "in" that key.

Key Signature Rules:

1. Read/write the key signature between the clef and the time signature.

2. Use sharps, flats, and the lack of sharps and flats to show the key of music.

3. Each accidental has a particular line or space it is always written on for key signatures. F# in a key signature for treble clef is always written on Line 5.

4. When an accidental is on a line or space of a key signature, it changes all notes of that pitch class. # on Line 5 in the key signature means **all** octave registers of F are written, read, and performed as F#s.

5. Natural accidentals can cancel the key signature for up to one measure at a time.

6. The only time you will write the same accidental as the key signature in your music is to change back from another accidental or as a courtesy accidental.

No Accidentals: Key of C Major   **One Sharp: Key of G Major**

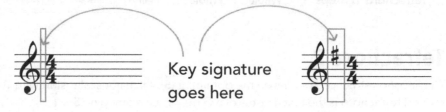

Key signature goes here

How to Use Accidentals in Key Signatures

Incorrect

No accidentals are needed for any F# because there is an F# in the key signature.

Correct

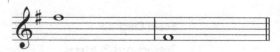

Because there is an F# in the key signature, the pitch class of F is sharp. All F notes are F# unless changed by a ♮ or ♭ accidental.

How to Identify Key Signatures:

The sharp that is the furthest from the clef (all the way to the right) is on the line or space for scale degree $\hat{7}$. In the key of G major, there is only one sharp—F. F is $\hat{7}$ of a G major scale.

$\hat{7}$ $\hat{1}$

34 **How to Write Key Signatures**

C Major

1. The C major scale has no accidentals, so the key signature also has no accidentals. This is the easiest key signature to write, because you don't need to write anything!

2. Write a treble clef.

3. Write the key signature.

4. Write the time signature.

G Major

1. The G major scale has one accidental on $\hat{7}$. Show the F# in the key signature with a # on Line 5.

2. Write a treble clef.

3. Write the key signature.

4. Write the time signature.

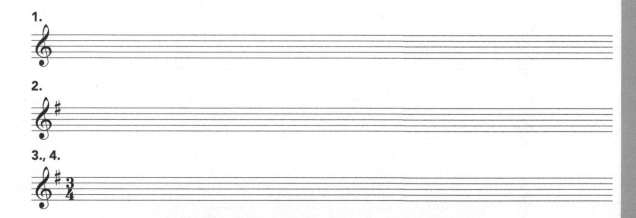

> **Reminder: Always write the # for the key signature of G major on Line 5 of the staff.**

35 How to Write Major Scales with Key Signatures:

1. Write a treble clef and a double bar line on a single line of staff.

2. Write the key signature.

3. Ascending scales: Write the first note of the scale on C4, C5, G3, or G4.

4. Descending scales: Write the first note of the scale on C5, C6, G4, or G5.

5. Write notes with no accidentals on every space and line, including the pitch class one octave higher or lower than the note you started on.

How to Write an Ascending C Major Scale with a Key Signature

How to Write an Ascending G Major Scale with a Key Signature

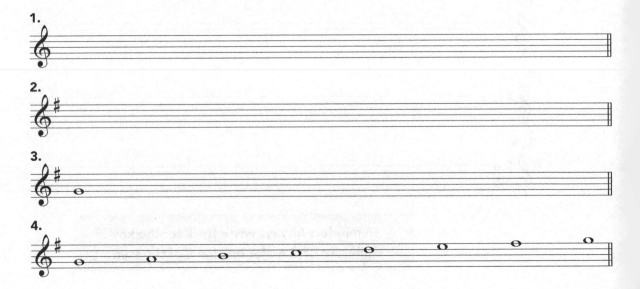

How to Write Descending Major Scales with a Key Signature

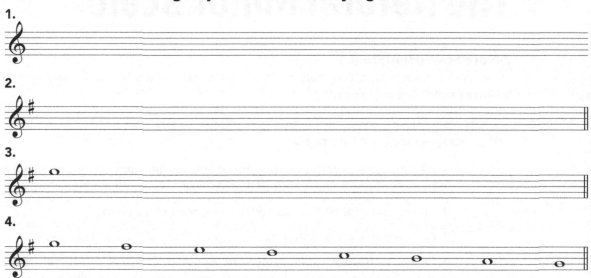

How to Write Ascending + Descending Major Scales with a Key Signature

1. Write a treble clef and a double bar line on a single line of staff.

2. Write the key signature.

3. Write the first note of the scale on C4, C5, G3, or G4.

4. Write notes with no accidentals on every space and line, including the pitch class one octave higher than the note you started on and on every space and line back down to the note you started on.

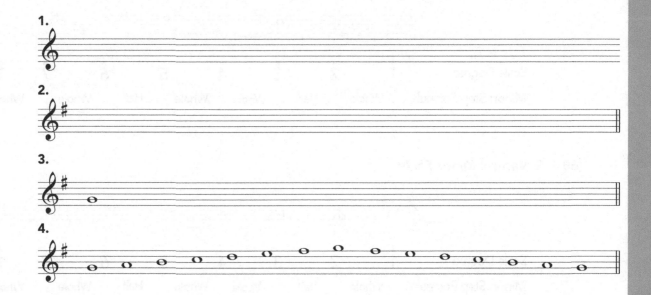

The Natural Minor Scale

7-Note Scale (Heptatonic)

The natural minor scale is called "natural" because the order of whole and half steps are the same as the major scale...but with a twist!

Natural Minor Scale Rules:

1. All natural minor scales can be understood, written, and performed with a minor step formula of whole and half steps (Whole, Half, Whole, Whole, Half, Whole, Whole).

2. Begins and ends on the same pitch class, one octave apart.

3. Natural minor scales can start on any note of the full musical alphabet.

4. One of each letter is used in the scale (one A, B, C, D, E, F, and G) before the pitch class that the scale started on repeats, which is the same as with major scales.

5. Either sharps or flats are used in a natural minor scale. Natural minor scales don't have both sharp and flat accidentals.

6. The Minor Step Formula stays the same for all natural minor scales.

7. The first whole step happens between $\hat{1}$ and $\hat{2}$.

Learn why scale degrees $\hat{3}$, $\hat{6}$, and $\hat{7}$ have a ♭ accidental on the next page.

---

(67) A Natural Minor Scale

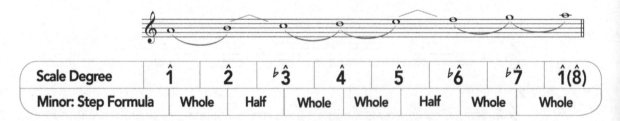

Scale Degree	$\hat{1}$	$\hat{2}$	♭$\hat{3}$	$\hat{4}$	$\hat{5}$	♭$\hat{6}$	♭$\hat{7}$	$\hat{1}(\hat{8})$
Minor: Step Formula	Whole	Half	Whole	Whole	Half	Whole	Whole	

(68) E Natural Minor Scale

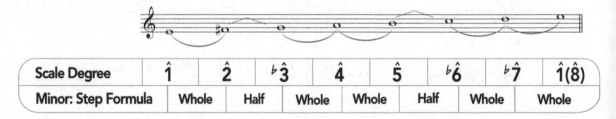

Scale Degree	$\hat{1}$	$\hat{2}$	♭$\hat{3}$	$\hat{4}$	$\hat{5}$	♭$\hat{6}$	♭$\hat{7}$	$\hat{1}(\hat{8})$
Minor: Step Formula	Whole	Half	Whole	Whole	Half	Whole	Whole	

Natural Minor Scales: Rules and Accidentals for E Natural Minor Scale (Example (68))

Rule 4: $\hat{2}$ is not G♭. There is already "some kind of" G on ♭$\hat{3}$.

Rule 6: To keep the formula of whole and half-steps, $\hat{2}$ is raised up with an accidental. If it was left as an F♮ that would not work with the formula—that would make a half step instead of a whole step.

Compare Major and Minor

Major scales have a happy, easy sound. Minor scales have a sad, thoughtful sound. Compare the sounds of ⑥⑤ G major and ⑥⑧ E natural minor scales. Can you hear that the G major scale sounds happy? Can you hear that the E natural minor scale sounds sad?

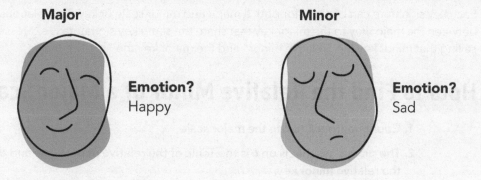

Major		Minor	
	Emotion? Happy		Emotion? Sad

Compare Major and Natural Minor Scales; Scale Quality

Scale quality is the word "major" or the word "minor" that we use in the scale name.
The quality of a C major scale is **major.** The quality of an A natural minor scale is **natural minor.**

Natural Minor Scale Degrees

Lowering Scale Degrees by One Half-Step

The ♭ accidental on scale degrees $\hat{3}$, $\hat{6}$, and $\hat{7}$ of the natural minor scale is because $\hat{3}$, $\hat{6}$, and $\hat{7}$ are one half-step lower than they are in the major scale. Scale degree accidentals show the distance between whole and half steps. Scale degrees do not show letter names or accidentals for the notes of the scale.

Major Scale Degrees

$\hat{1}$		$\hat{2}$		$\hat{3}$	$\hat{4}$		$\hat{5}$		$\hat{6}$		$\hat{7}$ $\hat{1}(\hat{8})$
Whole		Whole		Half	Whole		Whole		Whole		Half
Whole		Half		Whole	Whole		Half		Whole		Whole
$\hat{1}$		$\hat{2}$	♭$\hat{3}$		$\hat{4}$		$\hat{5}$	♭$\hat{6}$		♭$\hat{7}$	$\hat{1}(\hat{8})$

Natural Minor Scale Degrees

③⑥ Scale Degrees That Remain Unchanged

Scale degrees $\hat{1}$, $\hat{2}$, $\hat{4}$, and $\hat{5}$ remain unchanged.

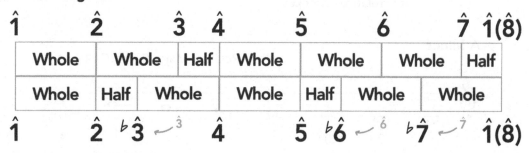

The ♭$\hat{3}$, ♭$\hat{6}$, and ♭$\hat{7}$ are flat <u>because of the change in the step formula</u>.
In the E major scale, $\hat{3}$ is G♯ because whole whole - E (W) F♯ (W) G♯ -
In the E minor scale, ♭$\hat{3}$ is G because whole half   - E (W) F♯ (H) G -
Accidentals in scale degrees show the <u>steps</u>, not the accidentals of the notes.

Relative Scales and Keys

Relative scales and keys share the same key signature and notes, but start on different Tonic notes.

What Are Relative Scales and Keys?

Each key signature can be used for both a major and minor scale or key. The relationship between the major key to the minor key that share the same key signature is expressed by calling that minor key the "relative minor" and the major key the "relative major."

How to Find the Relative Minor of a Major Scale or Key:

1. Count up from $\hat{1}$ to $\hat{6}$ in the major scale.

2. The pitch class that is on $\hat{6}$ is the Tonic of the relative minor scale and the letter name of the relative minor key.

C Major

How to Find the Relative Major of a Minor Scale or Key:

1. Count up from $\hat{1}$ to $\flat\hat{3}$ in the minor scale.

2. The pitch class that is on $\flat\hat{3}$ is the Tonic of the relative major scale and the letter name of the relative major key.

A Minor

Relative Scales and Keys: Major Perspective

It is best to use the major scale as the foundation for thinking further about the relationship between the relative major and minor keys. You will use the major scale as the foundation for understanding many more concepts in this and future books. The major scale is not better or superior; it is just a good starting point.

Relative Scales and Keys: Common Notes

Relative scales and keys share the same notes. The notes are presented in a different order.

Common Notes: C Major Scale and A Natural Minor Scale

C Major Notes	C	D	E	F	G	A	B
A Minor Notes	A	B	C	D	E	F	G

Common Notes: G Major Scale and E Natural Minor Scale

G Major Notes	G	A	B	C	D	E	F$^\#$
E Minor Notes	E	F$^\#$	G	A	B	C	D

Relative Scales and Keys: Scale Degrees

Think about the relative minor scale by taking scale degrees 6 and 7 of a major scale and putting them at the beginning of the scale.

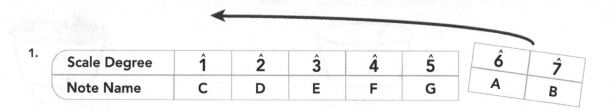

1.

Scale Degree	$\hat{1}$	$\hat{2}$	$\hat{3}$	$\hat{4}$	$\hat{5}$	$\hat{6}$	$\hat{7}$
Note Name	C	D	E	F	G	A	B

2.

Scale Degree	$\hat{6}$	$\hat{7}$	$\hat{1}$	$\hat{2}$	$\hat{3}$	$\hat{4}$	$\hat{5}$
Note Name	A	B	C	D	E	F	G

3.

Scale Degree	$\hat{6}$	$\hat{7}$	$\hat{1}$	$\hat{2}$	$\hat{3}$	$\hat{4}$	$\hat{5}$
Note Name	A	B	C	D	E	F	G

Renumber the scale degrees so that $\hat{6}$ is now $\hat{1}$ and you see the relative minor. You can do this with any major scale to find the relative minor. Reminder: the reason for the $\flat$ accidental on scale degrees $\hat{3}$, $\hat{6}$, and $\hat{7}$ of the natural minor scale is because $\flat\hat{3}$, $\flat\hat{6}$, and $\flat\hat{7}$ are all one half-step lower than they are in the major scale with the natural minor formula of W, H, W, W, H, W, W.

4.

Scale Degree	$\hat{1}$	$\hat{2}$	$\flat\hat{3}$	$\hat{4}$	$\hat{5}$	$\flat\hat{6}$	$\flat\hat{7}$
Note Name	A	B	C	D	E	F	G

Relative Scales and Keys: Key Signatures

Key signatures are like buckets. A key signature shows all the notes in a scale. We take all the notes from a scale, throw them in the bucket (key). All the notes in the scale are shown in the key signature.

C Major/A Minor Key Signature

There are no accidentals in the key signature because none of the notes have sharps or flats.

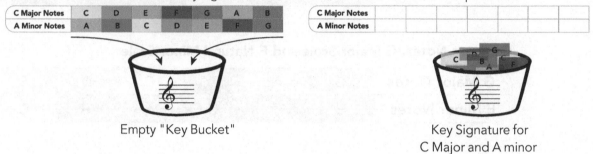

Empty "Key Bucket"　　　　　　Key Signature for
　　　　　　　　　　　　　　　　C Major and A minor

G Major/E Minor Key Signature

There is one accidental in the key signature because the F is F# in both relative scales.

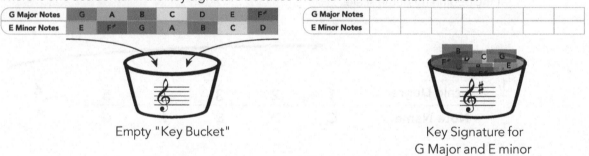

Empty "Key Bucket"　　　　　　Key Signature for
　　　　　　　　　　　　　　　　G Major and E minor

Because the notes of all relative major and minor scales are exactly the same, the key signature for relative keys and scales are the same. The key signature is showing all the notes in the "key" bucket.

37 Relative Step Formula

The same as you can think about moving scale degree $\hat{6}$ back to the beginning of the scale to get the relative minor, you can think about the major step formula to find relative minor scales.

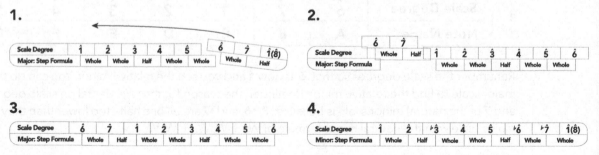

After moving $\hat{6}$ back to the beginning of the scale, renumber the scale degrees to show the natural minor.

How to Write Nat. Minor Scales

How to Write Natural Minor Scales with Accidentals

> **How to Write Ascending Natural Minor Scales with Accidentals**
>
> 1. Write a treble clef and a double bar line on a single line of staff.
>
> 2. Write the first note of the scale on A3, A4, E3, or E4.
>
> 3. Write notes with no accidentals on every space and line, including the pitch class one octave higher than the note you started on.
>
> 4. Label the Natural Minor Step Formula, using the curved lines for whole steps below the notes and angled lines (a roof or caret) for half steps (optional).
>
> 5. Add accidentals to make notes correct according to the Natural Minor Step Formula.

1.

2.

3.

4.

5.

> **How to Write Descending Natural Minor Scales with Accidentals**
>
> 1. Write a treble clef and a double bar line on a single line of staff.
>
> 2. Write the first note of the scale on A5, A4, E5, or E4.
>
> 3. Write notes with no accidentals on every space and line, including the pitch class one octave lower than the note you started on.
>
> 4. Label the Natural Minor Step Formula (optional).
>
> 5. Add accidentals to make notes correct according to the Natural Minor Step Formula.

How to Write Descending Natural Minor Scales with Accidentals

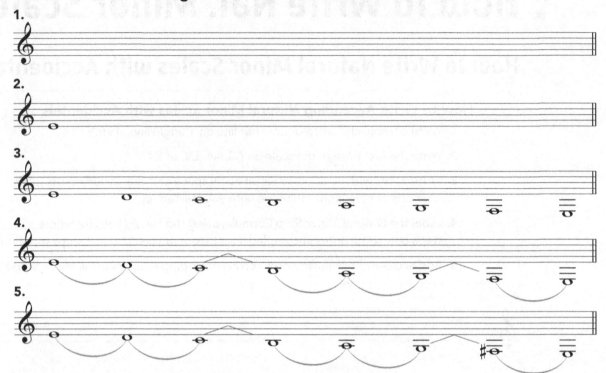

How to Write Ascending + Descending Natural Minor Scales with Accidentals

1. Write a treble clef and a double bar line on a single line of staff and the first note of the scale on any octave register of A or E.

2. Write notes with no accidentals on every space and line, including the pitch class one octave higher than the note you started on and on every space and line back down to the note you started on.

3. Label the Natural Minor Step Formula (optional).

4. Add in the accidentals needed to make each note the correct distance from the last according to the Natural Minor Step Formula with courtesy accidentals.

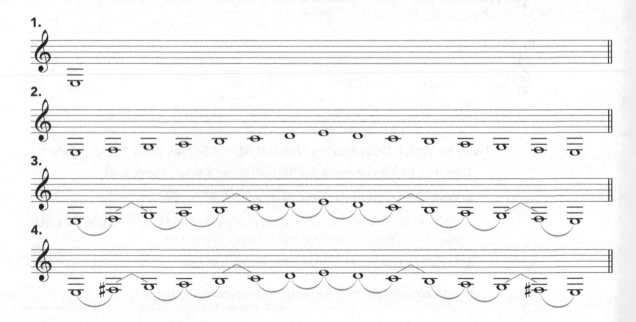

How to Write Natural Minor Scales with Key Signatures

1. Write a treble clef and a double bar line on a single line of staff.

2. Write the key signature.

3. Ascending: Write the first note of the scale on A3, A4, E3, or E4.

4. Descending: Write the first note of the scale on A5, A4, E5, or E4.

5. Write notes with no accidentals on every space and line, including the pitch class one octave higher or lower than the note you started on.

How to Write an Ascending E Natural Minor Scale with a Key Signature

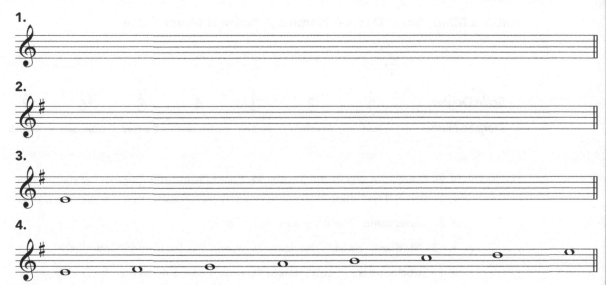

How to Write a Descending E Natural Minor Scale with a Key Signature

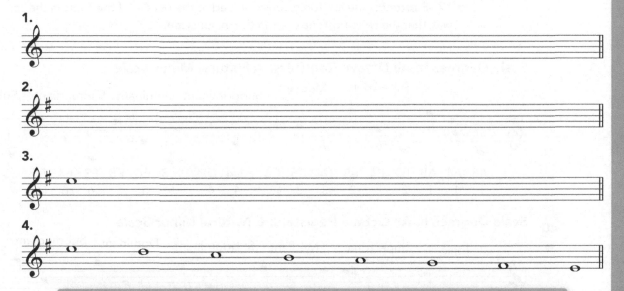

Follow the same steps for the ascending + descending natural minor scales.

Natural Minor Scale Degree Names

Natural Minor Scale Degree Rules:

1. Each scale degree has a name in addition to its assigned number.

2. The name of a scale degree describes the function of the note in the scale.

3. The scale degree names are the same for all natural minor scales.

4. Scale degrees apply to the pitch class of the note in **any** octave register.

Natural Minor Scale Degree Names: A Natural Minor Scale

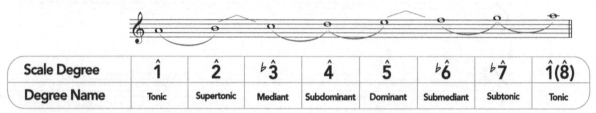

Scale Degree	$\hat{1}$	$\hat{2}$	$\flat\hat{3}$	$\hat{4}$	$\hat{5}$	$\flat\hat{6}$	$\flat\hat{7}$	$\hat{1}(\hat{8})$
Degree Name	Tonic	Supertonic	Mediant	Subdominant	Dominant	Submediant	Subtonic	Tonic

- **$\hat{1}$ - Tonic** - the first scale degree. This is the note that gives the scale its name. If the Tonic is an A, the scale is an A natural minor scale. **$\hat{8}$** is also the Tonic.

- **$\hat{2}$ - Supertonic** - The note above the Tonic.

- **$\flat\hat{3}$ - Mediant** - divides the notes between the Tonic and Dominant.

- **$\hat{4}$ - Subdominant** - "sub" means "below"; one note below the Dominant.

- **$\hat{5}$ - Dominant** - the second-most important note after the Tonic.

- **$\flat\hat{6}$ - Submediant** - divides the notes between Dominant and the octave of the Tonic.

- **$\flat\hat{7}$ - Subtonic** - the Subtonic does not lead to the octave of the Tonic in the same way that the Leading Tone does in the major scale.

Scale Degrees in All Octave Registers: A Natural Minor Scale

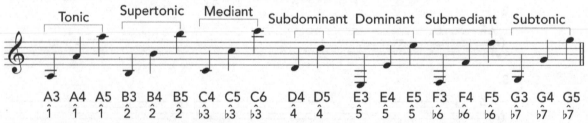

Scale Degrees in All Octave Registers: E Natural Minor Scale

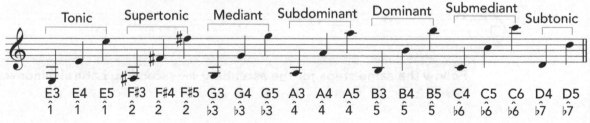

(69) Pentachord

"Penta" means five. A pentachord is a group of any five notes. The pentachords on this page are made with consecutive notes, starting on $\hat{1}$. In general, a pentachord will be the first five notes of the major or natural minor scales.

Why Do I Need to Know about Pentachords?

Pentachords are a quick way of distilling the basic differences between major and minor down to a simple five-note comparison. You will use this quick comparison to figure out the key of written music.

Major Pentachord

C Major Pentachord

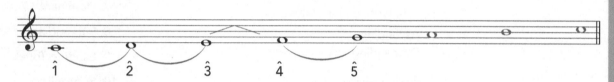

$\hat{1}$ $\hat{2}$ $\hat{3}$ $\hat{4}$ $\hat{5}$

(41) Minor Pentachord

A Minor Pentachord

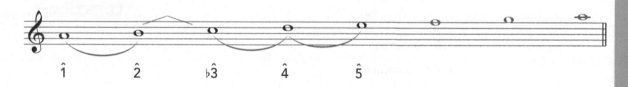

$\hat{1}$ $\hat{2}$ $\flat\hat{3}$ $\hat{4}$ $\hat{5}$

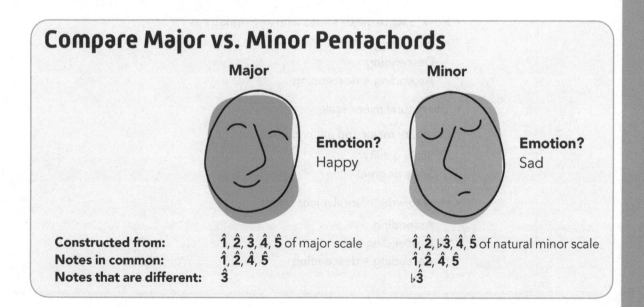

Compare Major vs. Minor Pentachords

	Major	Minor
	Emotion? Happy	Emotion? Sad
Constructed from:	$\hat{1}, \hat{2}, \hat{3}, \hat{4}, \hat{5}$ of major scale	$\hat{1}, \hat{2}, \flat\hat{3}, \hat{4}, \hat{5}$ of natural minor scale
Notes in common:	$\hat{1}, \hat{2}, \hat{4}, \hat{5}$	$\hat{1}, \hat{2}, \hat{4}, \hat{5}$
Notes that are different:	$\hat{3}$	$\flat\hat{3}$

Review: Pitch and Notes 3

- Chromatic scale
- How to write chromatic scales

    How to write a chromatic scale with flats
    How to write a chromatic scale with sharps

- Scale degrees

    Why we use scale degrees
    How to identify scale degrees
    What happens to the starting pitch class?
    How to write scale degrees

- Diatonic major scales
- How to write major scales

    Ascending
    Descending

- Scale degree names

    Tonic
    Supertonic
    Mediant
    Subdomiant
    Dominant
    Submediant
    Leading Tone

- Tetrachords
- Key signatures 1
    How to identify key signatures
    How to write key signatures

- How to write major scales with key signatures

    Ascending
    Descending
    Ascending + descending

- The natural minor scale
- Compare major and minor scales

    Scale quality
    Scale degrees

- How to write natural minor scales

    Ascending
    Descending
    Ascending + descending

New Words You Should Know

1. Scale
2. Chromatic
3. Tonic
4. Supertonic
5. Mediant
6. Subdomiant
7. Dominant
8. Submediant
9. Leading Tone
10. Subtonic
11. Key signature
12. Scale quality
13. Relative keys
14. Tetrachord
15. Pentachord

Pitch and Notes 4: Simple Intervals

Simple intervals are the foundation for many cool things like chords, the relationship between notes, melodies, and oh, so much more!

Simple Intervals

An interval is the distance between two notes. An interval is "simple" when it is an octave or smaller than an octave.

Melodic vs. Harmonic Intervals

 Melodic Intervals

There are two types of melodic intervals:

Ascending (Low to High)

Ascending intervals measure the distance from a low-sounding note to a high-sounding note.

Descending (High to Low)

Descending intervals measure the distance from a high-sounding note to a low-sounding note.

Harmony: Quick Definition

When two or more notes sound (happen) at the same time.

 Harmonic Intervals

Harmonic intervals are not ascending or descending. They are different because one note does not happen first to give context to the note that follows. Harmonic intervals are called "harmonic."

Major and Minor Intervals

Until now, you have used the terms major and minor to describe the quality of a scale or pentachord.

Minor Intervals

In the same way the natural minor scale has scale degrees ♭$\hat{3}$, ♭$\hat{6}$, and ♭$\hat{7}$, with intervals, "minor" means that we are lowering a note by one half-step compared to major intervals. Just like with scale degrees, whole and half-steps are what matter and it does not matter if the notes have accidentals.

Major Intervals

The term "major" will mean that the interval remains unchanged from the major scale and is not lowered by one half step. Many times in music theory we will use the major scale as the building block to understand and create other music.

Interval Quality 1

Major Intervals = M

Major intervals align with $\hat{2}$, $\hat{3}$, $\hat{6}$, and $\hat{7}$ of the major scale.
2nds, 3rds, 6ths, and 7ths can be major. Say "second," "third," "sixth," and "seventh."

C to D	C to E		C to A	C to B
M2	M3		M6	M7

Minor Intervals = m

Minor intervals are one half-step smaller than major intervals.
2nds, 3rds, 6ths, and 7ths can be minor. Say "second," "third," "sixth," and "seventh."

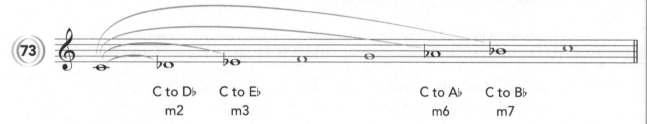

C to D♭	C to E♭		C to A♭	C to B♭
m2	m3		m6	m7

Perfect Intervals = P

Perfect intervals are $\hat{1}$, $\hat{4}$, and $\hat{5}$ of the major scale. Unisons, octaves, 4ths, and 5ths are perfect. Say "unison," "fourth," "fifth," and "octave." Unison intervals are two notes of the same pitch class and the same octave register. Perfect unison (PU) intervals are not ascending or descending; they are melodic or harmonic. More on unisons on the next page.

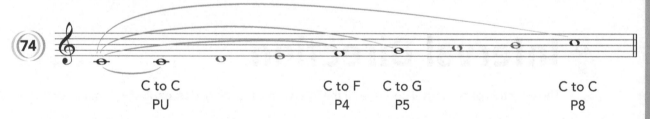

C to C		C to F	C to G		C to C
PU		P4	P5		P8

Augmented Intervals = A

Perfect intervals raised by one half-step.

Diminished Intervals = d

Perfect intervals lowered by one half-step.

The tritone is an interval that can be called A4 or d5, depending on the context. Every major scale has a tritone between scale degrees $\hat{4}$ and $\hat{7}$. It is called a tritone because the interval is a distance of three whole tones (three whole steps). B to F is 2 half-steps + 2 whole-steps = 3 whole steps.

F to B	B to F
A4	d5

Interval Quality 2

Interval quality is used to sort intervals by the way they sound.

Major Intervals = M	2, 3, 6, 7
Minor Intervals = m	2, 3, 6, 7
Perfect Intervals = P	U, 4, 5, 8
Augmented Intervals = A	4
Diminished Intervals = d	5

Introduction: Traditional Consonance and Dissonance

In the same way that a melody can be "pleasing" to you but not to someone else, what makes intervals consonant or dissonant can change for different people. In modern music "consonance" and "dissonance" can have more nuance than what you are about to learn. The information that follows is based on older, European/Western music traditions that still have value and show up in modern music—just not all the time. We will call this older way of thinking "traditional" consonance and dissonance.

A **consonant interval** is pleasing, harmonious, and does not have much friction. A consonant interval is stable and does not have tensions that may want to lead to resolution.

A **dissonant interval** is unsettling and full of friction. A dissonant interval is unstable and releases its tension by resolving, moving—or changing to a consonant interval.

Compare Traditional Consonance vs. Dissonance

Consonance	PU, P4, P5, P8, m3, M3, m6, M6
Dissonance	m2, M2, m7, M7, A4, d5

Can you hear the difference between the consonant and dissonant intervals in ⑦², ⑦³, and ⑦⁴?

42 Interval Direction

The direction of an interval describes if the interval is ascending, descending, harmonic, or unison.

Ascending (Low to High) asc.
Write "asc.," say "ascending."

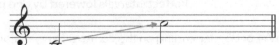

Descending (High to Low) dsc.
Write "dsc.," say "descending."

Harmonic Intervals hrm.
Write "hrm.," say "harmonic."

Unison Intervals U
Write U, say "unison." hrm. U = harmonic unisons. *Melodic unisons do not get a label of asc. or dsc.*

Interval Distance

Picking the correct enharmonic equivalent is important for naming and understanding interval quality, as is understanding how to calculate the distance from one note to another. Use the following tips to correctly name intervals.

1. Use the Basic Musical Alphabet: Some Kind Of...

Without calculating or thinking about sharps or flats or scale degrees, count up or down the basic musical alphabet, counting the note you start on as 1. These numbers are not scale degrees.

Ascending Intervals: Count Up the Basic Musical Alphabet

Example 1. C to D♭ ascending is "some kind of second" because C is 1 and D is 2.
Example 2. G to D♭ ascending is "some kind of fifth" because if we start on G and call it 1, A is 2, B is 3, C is 4, and D is 5.

1. C up to F is some kind of: **2.** C up to A is some kind of:

3. G up to A is some kind of: **4.** G up to C is some kind of:

Descending Intervals: Count Down the Basic Musical Alphabet

Example 1. D to C descending is "some kind of second" because if we start on D and call it 1, C is 2.
Example 2. G to D descending is "some kind of fourth" because if we start on G and call it 1, F is 2, E is 3, and F is 4.

1. C down to F is some kind of: **2.** C down to A is some kind of:

3. G down to A is some kind of: **4.** G down to C is some kind of:

Harmonic Intervals: Count Up the Basic Musical Alphabet

Just like ascending intervals, count up from the lowest to highest note for harmonic intervals, even though harmonic intervals are two notes happening at the same time.

Example 1. C to D harmonic is "some kind of second" because C is 1 and D is 2.
Example 2. G to D harmonic is "some kind of fifth" because if we start on G and call it 1, A is 2, B is 3, C is 4, and D is 5.

1. C up to G is some kind of: **2.** C up to B is some kind of:

3. G up to B is some kind of: **4.** G up to E is some kind of:

2. Add in Interval Quality

Use the "Simple Intervals: The Full Picture" diagram on p. 106 to figure out the possible qualities for your "some kind of" interval.

After "Some Kind Of..." Count Half Steps

After you know the "some kind of..." interval you are trying to read, write, or understand, count the half steps between both notes in the interval and compare that to the chart below to figure out or confirm the quality of the interval. How do you know if "some kind of second" is M or m? Count the half steps.

Memorize the number of half steps for m2 (1), M2 (2), m3 (3), and M3 (4).

Simple Intervals: The Full Picture

Ascending + Harmonic Intervals

Interval name	Notation	Number of Half Steps	Number of Whole Steps	Example/Pitch Class
Perfect Unison	PU	0	0	C - C
Ascending Minor Second	asc m2	1	.5	C - D♭
Ascending Major Second	asc M2	2	1	C - D
Ascending Minor Third	asc m3	3	1.5	C - E♭
Ascending Major Third	asc M3	4	2	C - E
Ascending Perfect Fourth	asc P4	5	2.5	C - F
Ascending Augmented Fourth /Diminished Fifth/Tritone	asc A4/d5	6	3	C-F#/C-G♭
Ascending Perfect Fifth	asc P5	7	3.5	C - G
Ascending Minor Sixth	asc m6	8	4	C - A♭
Ascending Major Sixth	asc M6	9	4.6	C - A
Ascending Minor Seventh	asc m7	10	5	C - B♭
Ascending Major Seventh	asc M7	11	5.5	C - B
Ascending Perfect Octave	asc P8	12	6	C - C

Descending Intervals

Interval name	Notation	Number of Half Steps	Number of Whole Steps	Example/Pitch Class
Perfect Unison	PU	0	0	C - C
Descending Minor Second	dsc m2	1	.5	C - B
Descending Major Second	dsc M2	2	1	C - B♭
Descending Minor Third	dsc m3	3	1.5	C - A
Descending Major Third	dsc M3	4	2	C - A♭
Descending Perfect Fourth	dsc P4	5	2.5	C - G
Descending Augmented Fourth /Diminished Fifth/Tritone	dsc A4/d5	6	3	C-G♭/C-F#
Descending Perfect Fifth	dsc P5	7	3.5	C - F
Descending Minor Sixth	dsc m6	8	4	C - E♭
Descending Major Sixth	dsc M6	9	4.5	C - E
Descending Minor Seventh	dsc m7	10	5	C - D
Descending Major Seventh	dsc M7	11	5.5	C - D♭
Descending Perfect Octave	dsc P8	12	6	C - C

How to Name Simple Intervals

How to Name asc. & hrm. Intervals

1. Figure out interval direction. p. 104

2. Figure out the "some kind of" interval (use the **basic** musical alphabet; the lowest note is 1). p.105

3. Which qualities could be used for the "some kind of" interval distance? p.104

4. Figure out whole or half steps to know the quality of the interval (use the **full** musical alphabet). Compare with p.106.

5. Say or write the interval with direction, quality, and distance.

How to Name dsc. Intervals

1. Figure out interval direction. p. 104

2. Figure out the "some kind of" interval (use the **basic** musical alphabet; the highest note is 1). p. 105

3. Which qualities could be used for the "some kind of" interval distance? p.104

4. Figure out whole or half steps to know the quality of the interval (use the **full** musical alphabet). Compare with p.106.

5. Say or write the interval with direction, quality, and distance.

Summary:

1. Name the direction of the interval (asc., dsc., hrm.).

2. Name the quality of the interval (M, m, P, A, d).

3. Name the distance of the interval (U, 2, 3, 4, 5, 6, 7, 8).

Examples:

- C to a higher-sounding D♭ – say: "an ascending minor 2nd." Write: asc. m2.

- C to a lower-sounding B – say: "a descending minor 2nd." Write: dsc. m2.

- C and D played together – say: "a harmonic major 2nd." Write: hrm. M2.

44 Compare Intervals

If the lowest note of a hrm. or asc. interval is $\hat{1}$ (the tonic) of a major scale you know, you can quickly compare an interval that is different to the major scale to identify the quality of the interval.
Example 1: the F♯ (not in C major scale) raises the F that is a P4 up one half-step to make it an A4.
Example 2: the F♯ (not in C major scale) raises the F up one half-step to a d5, instead of a P5.
Example 3: the F♮ (not in G major scale) lowers the F♯ by one half-step to m7.
Example 4: the F♮ (not in G major scale) lowers the F♯ by one half-step to M2.

Example 1

asc. P4   asc. A4

Example 2

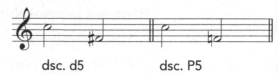

dsc. d5   dsc. P5

Example 3

asc. m7   asc. M7

Example 4

dsc. m2   dsc. M2

How to Write Simple Intervals

How to Write Simple Intervals: Melodic

How to Write Ascending Simple Intervals

1. Write a treble clef, a double bar line, and a starting note. Write the interval direction, quality, and distance you will be writing under the staff.

2. Count up the number of half and/or whole steps needed for the interval (See p. 106).

3. Write the next note to create the interval using accidentals as needed.

1.

2.

3.

asc. M6

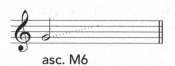

asc. M6

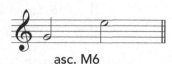

asc. M6

How to Write Descending Simple Intervals

1. Write a treble clef, a double bar line, and a starting note. Write the interval direction, quality, and distance you will be writing under the staff.

2. Count down the number of half and/or whole steps needed for the interval (See p. 106).

3. Write the next note to create the interval using accidentals as needed.

1.

2.

3.

dsc. M6

dsc. M6

dsc. M6

How to Write Simple Intervals: Harmonic

Harmonic Intervals: Noteheads

Harmonic Interval Notehead Rules:

1. Harmonic intervals are written with notes of the same rhythmic value.

2. For harmonic unisons, write both noteheads on either side of the stem.

3. For hrm. m2 and hrm. M2, write the lowest note facing to the left.

1.   **2.**   **3.**

Harmonic Intervals: Stems

You are now ready for some fun new ways of writing stems.

The Open End of Stems

The open end of the stem is the part of the stem that is furthest away from the noteheads.

Open End of the Stem

Open End of the Stem

Harmonic Interval Stem Rules:

1. Stem length is 4 staff lines long from the note closest to the open end of the stem.

2. If the notehead closest to the open end of the stem is on one ledger line (above or below the staff) the stem length remains 4 staff lines long.

3. If the notehead closest to the open end of the stem is past one ledger line (above or below the staff), the stem reaches Line 3 of the staff.

4. If the notehead furthest away from Line 3 of the staff is above Line 3: stem down.

5. If the notehead furthest away from Line 3 of the staff is below Line 3: stem up.

6. If the noteheads are the same distance from Line 3 of the staff: stem down.

How to Write Harmonic Simple Intervals

1. Write a treble clef, a double bar line, and a starting notehead. Write the interval direction, quality, and distance you will be writing under the staff.

2. Count up the number of half and/or whole steps needed for the interval (See p. 106).

3. Write the next notehead directly above the first note to create the interval using accidentals as needed.

4. Add a stem for half and quarter notes.

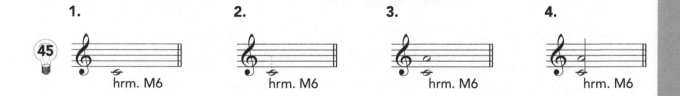

Review: Pitch and Notes 4

- Melodic intervals
    Ascending
    Descending

- Harmonic intervals

- Major and minor intervals

- Interval quality 1
    Major = M
    minor = m
    Perfect = P
    Augmented = A
    diminished = d
    Unison intervals
    Octave intervals

- Simple intervals: the full picture

- Interval quality 2
    Introduction: consonance and dissonance
    Perfect consonance
    Imperfect consonance

- Interval direction
    asc.
    dsc.
    hrm.

- Interval distance
    Ascending intervals
    Descending intervals
    Harmonic intervals

- How to name simple intervals

- How to write simple intervals: melodic
    How to write ascending simple intervals
    How to write descending simple intervals

- How to write simple intervals: harmonic
    Harmonic intervals: noteheads
    Harmonic intervals: stems

New Words You Should Know

1. Ascending
2. Descending
3. Melodic
4. Harmonic
5. Interval
6. Perfect
7. Augmented
8. Diminished
9. Unison
10. Consonance
11. Dissonance
12. Perfect consonance
13. Imperfect consonance
14. Interval quality
15. Interval type
16. Interval distance

Memorize the number of half steps for m2 (1), M2 (2), m3 (3), and M3 (4).

Harmony 1: Triads

Harmony is the foundation for creating, understanding, and analyzing various genres and styles.

Harmony

Harmony is when two or more notes happen at the same time. Notes are stacked on top of each other to make different sounds, just like harmonic intervals from the last chapter.

(76) Hear and See Harmony

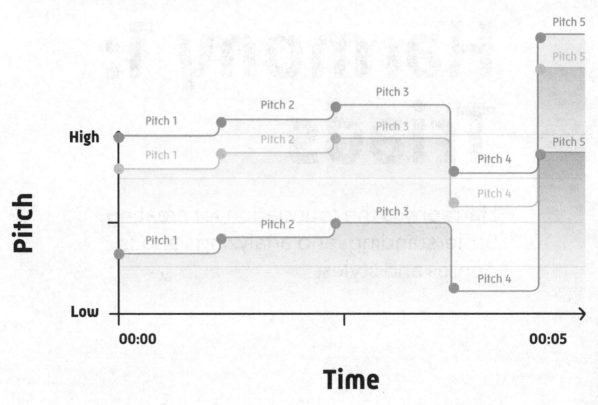

What Is a Chord?

A chord is harmony, and harmony makes chords. Chords are a way of giving names to and describing the quality of different harmonies.

Is It a Chord or an Interval?

There are two schools of thought on how to categorize harmonic intervals:

1. Any two notes sounded at the same time are an interval (true). They are not a chord (debatable).

2. Any two notes sounded at the same time can be classified as an interval and as a "dyad," which is a type of chord.

The idea of a chord is that it is a harmony that conveys feeling, emotion, and meaning. The argument is that if you only have two notes, that sound is not complex enough to imply feeling, emotion, and meaning.

What do you think? Do intervals convey emotion and meaning?

Triads

Triads are three-note chords that are created with particular intervals. There are other three-note chords that are **not** triads.

Chord Tones

Chord tones are the notes that are in a chord. Chord tones have names, just like scale degrees. **Chord tones are not scale degrees** but we can understand them with related scale degrees. We can quickly find chord tones for triads in the major and minor pentachord.

Root

Each chord starts on a note, called the "Root," which is the same note as $\hat{1}$.

Third

The Third is the same note as scale degrees $\hat{3}$ and $\flat\hat{3}$. $\flat\hat{3}$ does not mean the note is flat; it is three half-steps (m3) away from the Root (whole, half from the natural minor scale formula), not four half-steps (M3) (whole, whole from the major scale formula).

The Third in Minor Chords

Sometimes to be clear musicians will say "the flat Third" or "the flat 3" to differentiate between the Third of the major chord and a minor chord. These terms are not perfect, since they can also be used for scales, but they get the job done most of the time.

Fifth

The Fifth of the chord is related to $\hat{5}$.

(77) **Major Chord Tones: C Major**

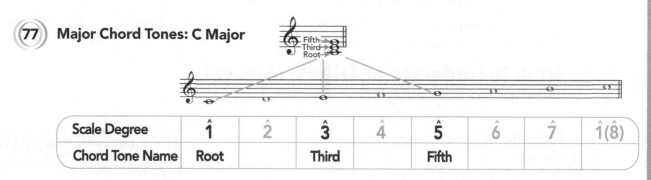

Scale Degree	$\hat{1}$	$\hat{2}$	$\hat{3}$	$\hat{4}$	$\hat{5}$	$\hat{6}$	$\hat{7}$	$\hat{1}(\hat{8})$
Chord Tone Name	Root		Third		Fifth			

(78) **Minor Chord Tones: A Minor**

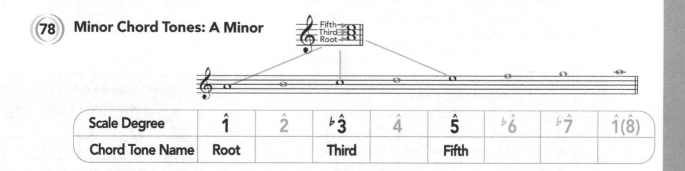

Scale Degree	$\hat{1}$	$\hat{2}$	$\flat\hat{3}$	$\hat{4}$	$\hat{5}$	$\flat\hat{6}$	$\flat\hat{7}$	$\hat{1}(\hat{8})$
Chord Tone Name	Root		Third		Fifth			

(79) Major vs. Minor Triads

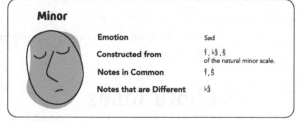

Major		
Emotion	Happy
Constructed from	$\hat{1}$, $\hat{3}$, $\hat{5}$ of the major scale
Notes in Common	$\hat{1}$, $\hat{5}$
Notes that are Different	$\hat{3}$

Minor		
Emotion	Sad
Constructed from	$\hat{1}$, $\flat\hat{3}$, $\hat{5}$ of the natural minor scale.
Notes in Common	$\hat{1}$, $\hat{5}$
Notes that are Different	$\flat\hat{3}$

How to Understand Major and Minor Triad Names

Triads are named after their Root note. When there is a letter like C or G, the chord quality is major. If someone asks you to perform or write a "C chord," you will perform or write a C **major** chord.
Letter = major chord.
Perform or write a minor triad if asked to perform or write an E **"minor."** Minor chords can also be written as Emin or Em. **E-** is the most common way of writing minor chords in modern music.
Letter + minus sign = minor chord.

How to Name a Triad:

1. Name the Root Note

The Root note or "Root" is the note that gives the chord its letter name.
A minor: A = Root. C major: C = Root. E minor: E = Root. G major: G = Root.

2. Name the Chord Quality

Chord quality defines whether a chord is major or minor. A-: the quality is minor.
C: the quality is major.

Chord Symbols (Always Capital Letters)

When you read or write the letter name and quality of a chord it is called a chord symbol.

How to Understand Triads: Intervals

This is how we can think about triads using intervals.

Major Triad

The quality of the chord is major.
Made from $\hat{1}$, $\hat{3}$, and $\hat{5}$ of a major scale.
There is an interval of a M3 from $\hat{1}$ (Root) to $\hat{3}$ (Third).
There is in interval of a m3 from $\hat{3}$ (Third) to $\hat{5}$ (Fifth).
There is an interval of a P5 from $\hat{1}$ (Root) to $\hat{5}$ (Fifth).
Chord symbol options: C

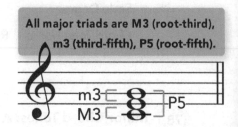

All major triads are M3 (root-third), m3 (third-fifth), P5 (root-fifth).

Minor Triad

The quality of the chord is minor.
Made from $\hat{1}$, $\flat\hat{3}$, and $\hat{5}$ of a natural minor scale.
There is an interval of a m3 from $\hat{1}$ (Root) to $\flat\hat{3}$ (Third).
There is in interval of a M3 from $\flat\hat{3}$ (Third) to $\hat{5}$ (Fifth).
There is an interval of a P5 from $\hat{1}$ (Root) to $\hat{5}$ (Fifth).
Chord symbol options: A-

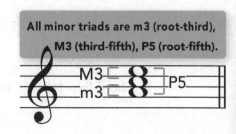

All minor triads are m3 (root-third), M3 (third-fifth), P5 (root-fifth).

(46)

How to Write Triads

Triad Stem Rules:

1. Stem length is 4 staff lines long from the notehead closest to the open end of the stem.

2. If the notehead closest to the open end of the stem is on one ledger line (above or below the staff), the stem length remains 4 staff lines long.

3. If the notehead closest to the open end of the stem is past one ledger line (above or below the staff), the stem reaches Line 3 of the staff.

4. If the outer notehead furthest away from Line 3 of the staff is above Line 3: stem down.

5. If the outer notehead furthest away from Line 3 of the staff is below Line 3: stem up.

6. If the outer noteheads are the same distance from Line 3 of the staff: stem down.

> The stem rules for triads are almost all the same as for intervals.

Outer Noteheads

How to Write Triads with Accidentals

1. Write a treble clef, double bar line, chord symbol, and Root note of the triad.

2. Write the Third of the triad with no accidentals:

   Root in a space: write the Third of the triad in the space above the Root.
   Root on a line: write the Third of the triad on the line above the Root.

3. Write the Fifth of the triad with no accidentals:

   Root in a space: write the Fifth of the triad in the space above the Third, two spaces above the Root.

   Root on a line: write the Fifth of the triad on the line above the Third, two lines above the Root.

4. Write in accidentals as needed to create the intervals to spell the desired chord.

5. Add stems for half and quarter notes. Your triad should look like a snowman.

Spaces

1.	2.	3.	4.	5.

Lines

1.	2.	3.	4.	5.

How to Write Triads with a Key Signature

1. Write a treble clef, key signature, double bar line, chord symbol, and Root of the triad.

2. Write the Third of the triad with no accidentals:

Root in a space: write the Third of the triad in the space above the Root.
Root on a line: write the Third of the triad on the line above the Root.

3. Write the Fifth of the triad with no accidentals:

Root in a space: write the Fifth of the triad in the space above the Third.
Root on a line: write the Fifth of the triad on the line above the Third.

4. Add stems for half and quarter notes.

Spaces

1.    **2.**    **3.**    **4.**

Lines

1.    **2.**    **3.**    **4.**

Dotted Note Triads

1. Follow single dotted note rules. Dots go in the same space for space notes and in the space above the note for line notes. Follow the same rules for notes on ledger lines.

2. Each note of the chord gets its own dot.

 ## Tied Note Triads

1. Two ties curve in the opposite direction of the stem, regardless of where the triad is written. **Stem down =** top two ties curve over. **Stem up =** bottom two ties curve under.

2. Flatten ties slightly to accommodate ledger lines. Ties should not touch ledger lines.

1.    **2.**

Triads: The Major Scale Harmonized to the Fifth

Harmonized Major Scales

1. A triad can be built (build a snowman) or written on every scale degree of any scale. This means you take any scale degree, call it the Root of a new triad, then write a Third and Fifth above that scale degree.

2. Each new triad uses notes from the scale for the Third and Fifth. When you harmonize a C major scale, you will only use notes from the C major scale in each triad. In the C major scale there are no accidentals. To harmonize a G major scale: all F notes are F♯s.

3. This is called "harmonizing" the scale.

4. Every harmonized major scale follows the same Major Scale Triad Quality Formula: Major, Minor, Minor, Major, Major, Minor for the first six notes of the scale.

5. The quality formula stays the same due to the way the intervals line up for each scale degree for all major scales. The triad on $\hat{3}$ is always minor. The triad on $\hat{5}$ is always major.

(80) C Major Scale Harmonized to the Fifth (the Fifth is the highest note of each chord)

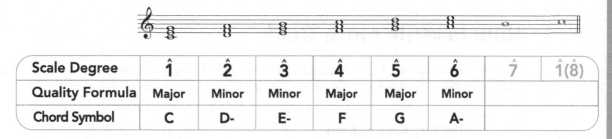

Scale Degree	$\hat{1}$	$\hat{2}$	$\hat{3}$	$\hat{4}$	$\hat{5}$	$\hat{6}$	$\hat{7}$	$\hat{1}(\hat{8})$
Quality Formula	Major	Minor	Minor	Major	Major	Minor		
Chord Symbol	C	D-	E-	F	G	A-		

New Major and Minor Triads: C Major

As you can see from the harmonized C major scale above, there are new triads like D-, E-, and F.

New Triad Rules

1. All major triads in all keys follow the same interval formula. M3 between Root and Third, m3 between Third and Fifth, and P5 between Root and Fifth.

2. All minor triads in all keys follow the same interval formula. m3 between Root and Third, M3 between Third and Fifth, and P5 between Root and Fifth.

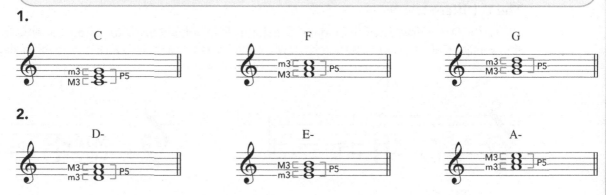

(81) G Major Scale Harmonized to the Fifth (the Fifth is the highest note of each chord)

Scale Degree	$\hat{1}$	$\hat{2}$	$\hat{3}$	$\hat{4}$	$\hat{5}$	$\hat{6}$	$\hat{7}$	$\hat{1}(\hat{8})$
Quality Formula	Major	Minor	Minor	Major	Major	Minor		
Chord Symbol	G	A-	B-	C	D	E-		

New Major and Minor Triads: G Major

As you can see from the harmonized G major scale above, with F#, there are new triads like B- and D.

1.

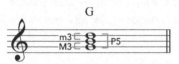
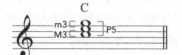
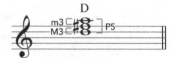

2.

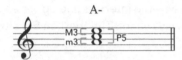
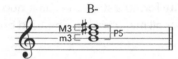

How to Write More Triads

While you can count the half steps for the m3 and M3 between the Root, Third, and Fifth of all the triads, just like with intervals, it is useful to relate these triads back to the major scale.

Triad Key Connections

There are four triads that show up in both C and G major.

C
Major triad starting on the tonic, $\hat{1}$ of C.
Major triad starting on the subdominant, $\hat{4}$ of G.

E-
Minor triad starting on the mediant, $\hat{3}$ of C.
Minor triad starting on the submediant, $\hat{6}$ of G.

G
Major triad starting on the dominant, $\hat{5}$ of C.
Major triad starting on the tonic, $\hat{1}$ of G.

A-
Minor triad starting on the submediant, $\hat{6}$ of C.
Minor triad starting on the supertonic, $\hat{2}$ of G.

The D Difference

Why is the D triad from harmonizing the C major scale minor, but the D triad from harmonizing the G major scale is major? It all comes down to the Third and if there is an F or F# in the scale.

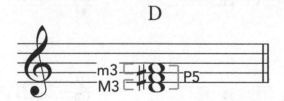
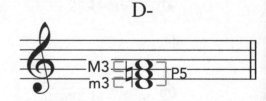

How to Write More Triads with Accidentals and Key Signatures

1. Write the Root of the triad and a "snowman" to add the Third and Fifth of the triad. Write ledger lines if needed. There are two ways you can think about accidentals.

2. Are there accidentals? **Option 1:** Which harmonized scale does this triad fit with?
   Option 2: Count half steps - Root to Third, then Third to Fifth.

   Example 1A: B- triad. You can think of B- as starting on the mediant of G. You know the quality is minor because of the quality formula and you know the F is sharp from the harmonized G major scale that the B- comes from. Add the accidental.
   Example 1B: You can think in terms of intervals, m3 from Root to Third, M3 from Third to Fifth, P5 from Root to Fifth. Count the half steps to check your work.

   Example 2A: C triad. Think of C as either tonic, 1̂ of C, or subdominant, 4̂ of G. You know the quality is major because of the quality formula for C and G harmonized scales and there are no accidentals because there are no F notes.
   Example 2B: You can think in terms of intervals, M3 from Root to Third, m3 from Third to Fifth, P5 from Root to Fifth. Count the half steps to check your work.

3. **Option 1:** Add in accidentals on any notes that have accidentals in the harmonized scale.
   Option 2: Add in accidentals because they are needed to make the correct intervals.

1.  **2.**  **3.**

48

> A chord or scale is "spelled" by listing the names of the chord tones, or notes in the scale, with any needed accidentals.

Major Scale Harmonized to the Fifth: Roman Numerals

Roman Numerals represent chord names, qualities, and which scale degree the chord is built on. Uppercase Roman Numerals show major triads. Lowercase Roman Numerals show minor triads. "Roman Numerals" is abbreviated as RN. RNs show the scale degree the triad starts on + triad quality.

Number	1	2	3	4	5	6	7	
Minor RNs	i	ii	iii	iv	v	vi	vii	
Major RNs	I	II	III	IV	V	VI	VII	

Roman Numerals Showing the Triad Quality Formula: Major

Major

I   IV V

Minor

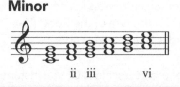

ii iii   vi

Triad Quality Formula

I ii iii IV V vi

> Sometimes uppercase major Roman Numerals do not have the horizontal line on the top and bottom; they are just larger. Always write them with the lines for clarity.

Scale Degree	$\hat{1}$	$\hat{2}$	$\hat{3}$	$\hat{4}$	$\hat{5}$	$\hat{6}$	$\hat{7}$	$\hat{1}(\hat{8})$
Quality Formula	Major	Minor	Minor	Major	Major	Minor		
Roman Numerals	I	ii	iii	IV	V	vi		
Key of C major	C	D-	E-	F	G	A-		
Key of G major	G	A-	B-	C	D	E-		

⑲ How to Write a Harmonized Major Scale to the Fifth

> ### How to Write a Harmonized Major Scale to the Fifth with Accidentals
>
> 1. Write a treble clef, double bar line, major scale up to $\hat{6}$, and chord symbols.
>
> 2. Write a "snowman" with a Third and Fifth of each triad on the lines or spaces above the Root for each note in the scale. Add ledger lines as needed.
>
> 3. Write accidentals and stems as needed, and use courtesy accidentals.
>
> 4. Optional and not shown: add Roman Numerals below the staff for each chord.

1.   **2.**   **3.**

G A- B- C D E-   G A- B- C D E-   G A- B- C D E-

> ### How to Write a Harmonized Major Scale to the Fifth with a Key Signature
>
> 1. Write a treble clef, key signature, double bar line, major scale up to $\hat{6}$, and chord symbols.
>
> 2. Write a "snowman" with a Third and Fifth of each triad on the lines or spaces above the Root for each note in the scale. Add ledger lines as needed.
>
> 3. Optional: add Roman Numerals below the staff for each chord.

1.   **2.**   **3.**

G A- B- C D E-   G A- B- C D E-   G A- B- C D E-

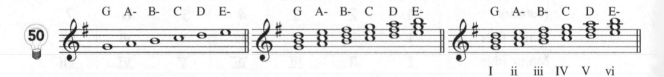

                                    I   ii   iii   IV   V   vi

Talking Triads and RNs

Musicians talk about Roman Numerals in a few ways. In the key of C, they might say: "the four" (F), "the five of the Tonic"(G)," the two of the Root"(D-). These ways of describing a chord get everyone to understand which chord is being talked about.

If you know the Tonic of the key/scale is G, you instantly know that ii is A-, iii is B-, and so on.

Triads: The Natural Minor Scale Harmonized to the Fifth

Harmonizing the Natural Minor Scale to the Fifth Rules:

1. A triad can be built (build a snowman), or written on every scale degree of any scale. This means you take any scale degree call it the Root of a new triad, then write a Third and Fifth above the scale degree.

2. Each triad uses only notes from the scale. For example, when you harmonize an A natural minor scale, you will only use notes from the A natural minor scale in each triad to figure out which accidentals to use.

3. This is called "harmonizing" the scale.

4. Every harmonized natural minor scale follows the same Natural Minor Scale Triad Quality Formula: Minor, SKIP, Major, Minor, Minor, Major, Major. (We will look at what happens on $\hat{2}$ in *The Best Music Theory Book for Beginners: 2*.)

5. The quality formula stays the same because of the way the intervals line up for each scale degree for all natural minor scales. The triad on $\flat\hat{3}$ is always major. The triad on $\hat{5}$ is always minor.

(82) **A Natural Minor Scale Harmonized to the Fifth**

Scale Degree	1	$\hat{2}$	$\flat\hat{3}$	$\hat{4}$	$\hat{5}$	$\flat\hat{6}$	$\flat\hat{7}$	$\hat{1}(\hat{8})$
Quality Formula	Minor		Major	Minor	Minor	Major	Major	
Chord Symbol	A-		C	D-	E-	F	G	

(51) (83) **E Natural Minor Scale Harmonized to the Fifth**

Scale Degree	$\hat{1}$	$\hat{2}$	$\flat\hat{3}$	$\hat{4}$	$\hat{5}$	$\flat\hat{6}$	$\flat\hat{7}$	$\hat{1}(\hat{8})$
Quality Formula	Minor		Major	Minor	Minor	Major	Major	
Chord Symbol	E-		G	A-	B-	C	D	

Relative Scales: Harmonized

How to Find the Relative Minor of a Major Key or Scale: Reminder

1. Count up from $\hat{1}$ to $\hat{6}$ in the major scale.

2. The pitch class that is on $\hat{6}$ is the letter name of the relative minor key/scale.

C Major

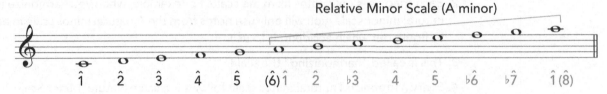

Relative Harmonized Scales: Scale Degrees

Just like the scales they come from are related in relative ways, the harmonized scales are also connected with the same relative relationship. Think about the relative minor by taking scale degrees 6 and 7 of a major scale and putting them at the beginning of the scale.

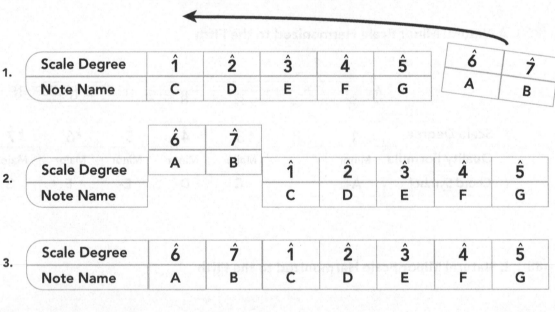

Renumber the scale degrees so that scale degree 6 is now scale degree 1 and it is the relative minor. You can do this with any major scale to find the relative minor. Reminder: the reason for the ♭ accidental on scale degrees $\hat{3}$, $\hat{6}$, and $\hat{7}$ of the natural minor scale is because ♭$\hat{3}$, ♭$\hat{6}$, and ♭$\hat{7}$ are all one half-step lower than they are in the major scale with the natural minor formula of W, H, W, W, H, W, W.

	Scale Degree	$\hat{1}$	$\hat{2}$	♭$\hat{3}$	$\hat{4}$	$\hat{5}$	♭$\hat{6}$	♭$\hat{7}$
4.	Note Name	A	B	C	D	E	F	G

Relative Harmonized Scales: Chords

Relative harmonized scales share the same chords because they share the same notes. No notes change between relative major and minor scales so the triads and chord qualities stay the same.

Harmonized C Major and A Natural Minor Have the Same Chords

Scale Degree	$\hat{1}$	$\hat{2}$	$\hat{3}$	$\hat{4}$	$\hat{5}$	$\hat{6}$	$\hat{7}$	$\hat{1}(\hat{8})$
Chord Symbol	C	D-	E-	F	G	A-		

Common Chords: C, D-, E-, F, G, A-

Scale Degree	$\hat{1}$	$\hat{2}$	$\flat\hat{3}$	$\hat{4}$	$\hat{5}$	$\flat\hat{6}$	$\flat\hat{7}$	$\hat{1}(\hat{8})$
Chord Symbol	A-		C	D-	E-	F	G	

Harmonized G Major and E Natural Minor Have the Same Chords

Scale Degree	$\hat{1}$	$\hat{2}$	$\hat{3}$	$\hat{4}$	$\hat{5}$	$\hat{6}$	$\hat{7}$	$\hat{1}(\hat{8})$
Chord Symbol	G	A-	B-	C	D	E-		

Common Chords: G, A-, B-, C, D, E-

Scale Degree	$\hat{1}$	$\hat{2}$	$\flat\hat{3}$	$\hat{4}$	$\hat{5}$	$\flat\hat{6}$	$\flat\hat{7}$	$\hat{1}(\hat{8})$
Chord Symbol	E-		G	A-	B-	C	D	

Relative Harmonized Keys: Triad Quality Formula

Move $\hat{6}$ back to the beginning of a major scale to create the Relative Minor Quality Formula.

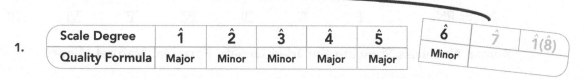

1.

Scale Degree	$\hat{1}$	$\hat{2}$	$\hat{3}$	$\hat{4}$	$\hat{5}$	$\hat{6}$	$\hat{7}$	$\hat{1}(\hat{8})$
Quality Formula	Major	Minor	Minor	Major	Major	Minor		

2.

Scale Degree	$\hat{6}$	$\hat{7}$	$\hat{1}$	$\hat{2}$	$\hat{3}$	$\hat{4}$	$\hat{5}$
Quality Formula	Minor		Major	Minor	Minor	Major	Major

The quality formula now matches the natural minor scale.

3.

Scale Degree	$\hat{6}$	$\hat{7}$	$\hat{1}$	$\hat{2}$	$\hat{3}$	$\hat{4}$	$\hat{5}$
Quality Formula	Minor		Major	Minor	Minor	Major	Major

Renumber the scale degrees so that $\hat{6}$ is now $\hat{1}$ to match the natural minor scale.

4.

Scale Degree	$\hat{1}$	$\hat{2}$	$\flat\hat{3}$	$\hat{4}$	$\hat{5}$	$\flat\hat{6}$	$\flat\hat{7}$	$\hat{1}(\hat{8})$
Quality Formula	Minor		Major	Minor	Minor	Major	Major	

How to Write Triads from the Natural Minor Scale

Natural Minor Scale Triads

Because of the relative relationship from major scales to natural minor scales, there are no new triads to learn. The triads are the same. The only change is that they are presented in a different order.

Harmonized C Major and A Natural Minor Have the Same Chords

Scale Degree	î	2̂	3̂	4̂	5̂	6̂	7̂	1̂(8)
Chord Symbol	C	D-	E-	F	G	A-		

Scale Degree	î	2̂	♭3̂	4̂	5̂	♭6̂	♭7̂	1̂(8)
Chord Symbol	A-		C	D-	E-	F	G	

Common Chords: C, D-, E-, F, G, A-

Harmonized G Major and E Natural Minor Have the Same Chords

Scale Degree	î	2̂	3̂	4̂	5̂	6̂	7̂	1̂(8)
Chord Symbol	G	A-	B-	C	D	E-		

Scale Degree	î	2̂	♭3̂	4̂	5̂	♭6̂	♭7̂	1̂(8)
Chord Symbol	E-		G	A-	B-	C	D	

Common Chords: G, A-, B-, C, D, E-

Natural Minor Scale Harmonized to the Fifth: Roman Numerals

Number	1	2	3	4	5	6	7	
Minor RNs	i	ii	iii	iv	v	vi	vii	
Major RNs	I	II	III	IV	V	VI	VII	

Roman Numerals Showing the Triad Quality Formula: Natural Minor

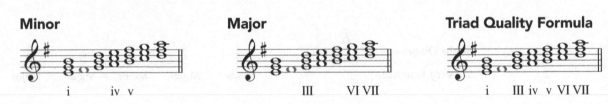

Minor	Major	Triad Quality Formula
i iv v	III VI VII	i III iv v VI VII

E Natural Minor Scale Harmonized to the Fifth + Roman Numerals

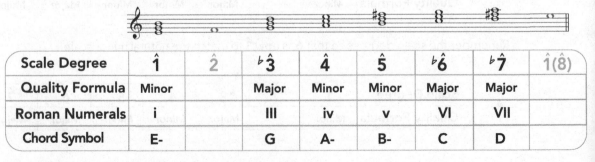

Scale Degree	î	2̂	♭3̂	4̂	5̂	♭6̂	♭7̂	1̂(8)
Quality Formula	Minor		Major	Minor	Minor	Major	Major	
Roman Numerals	i		III	iv	v	VI	VII	
Chord Symbol	E-		G	A-	B-	C	D	

A Natural Minor Scale Harmonized to the Fifth + Roman Numerals

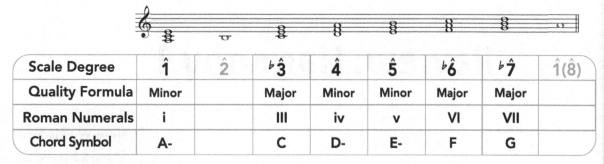

Scale Degree	$\hat{1}$	$\hat{2}$	$\flat\hat{3}$	$\hat{4}$	$\hat{5}$	$\flat\hat{6}$	$\flat\hat{7}$	$\hat{1}(\hat{8})$
Quality Formula	Minor		Major	Minor	Minor	Major	Major	
Roman Numerals	i		III	iv	v	VI	VII	
Chord Symbol	A-		C	D-	E-	F	G	

How to Write a Harmonized Natural Minor Scale to the Fifth

> **How to Write a Harmonized Natural Minor Scale to the Fifth with Accidentals**
>
> 1. Write a treble clef, double bar line, natural minor scale, and chord symbols, skipping $\hat{2}$.
>
> 2. Write a "snowman" with a Third and Fifth of each triad on the lines or spaces above the Root for each note in the scale. Add ledger lines as needed.
>
> 3. Write accidentals as needed, and use courtesy accidentals. Optional: add RNs.

1.

E- G A- B- C D

2.

E- G A- B- C D

3.

E- G A- B- C D

i   III iv v VI VII

> **How to Write a Harmonized Natural Minor Scale to the Fifth with a Key Signature**
>
> 1. Write a treble clef, key signature, double bar line, natural minor scale, and chord symbols, skipping $\hat{2}$.
>
> 2. Write a "snowman" with a Third and Fifth of each triad on the lines or spaces above the Root for each note in the scale. Add ledger lines as needed. Optional: add Roman Numerals below the staff for each chord.

1.

E- G A- B- C D

2.

E- G A- B- C D

i   III iv v VI VII

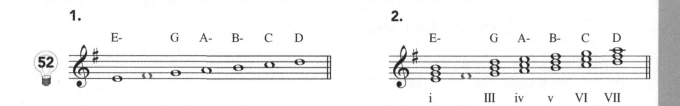

Review: Harmony 1

- Harmony
- What is a chord?
    Intervals
    Dyads
- Triads
- Chord tones
    Root
    Third
    Fifth
- Major vs. minor triads
- How to name a chord
    Root note
    Quality
- How to understand triads: intervals
- How to write triads
    Stem rules
    How to write triads with accidentals
    How to write triads with key signatures
- Triads: the major scale harmonized to the Fifth
- New triads
- Roman Numerals
- How to write a harmonized major scale to the Fifth
    How to write a harmonized major scale to the Fifth with accidentals
    How to write a harmonized major scale to the Fifth with a key signature
- Triads: the natural minor scale harmonized to the Fifth
- How to write a natural minor scale harmonized to the Fifth
    How to write a natural minor scale harmonized to the Fifth with accidentals
    How to write a natural minor scale harmonized to the Fifth with a key signature
- How to identify triads

New Words You Should Know

1. Harmony
2. Chord
3. Dyad
4. Triad
5. Chord tone
6. Root
7. Third
8. Fifth
9. Chord quality
10. Harmonized
11. Roman Numerals

Analysis 1: Degrees and Numerals

Put everything you have learned so far in this book to use for analysis and understanding music!

How to Analyze Lead Sheets

Lead sheets show a melody written in notation with chord symbols above the melody.

How to Read Lead Sheets

Chords

The chord symbols will be written above the staff. In the second measure of the example below, there is no chord symbol. This is because the G chord over measure 1 will last through every measure until a different chord symbol is written. Chord symbols apply to measures that have rests because the measures with rests are showing a silence in the melody, not the chords.

Chord symbols = last until the next chord symbol

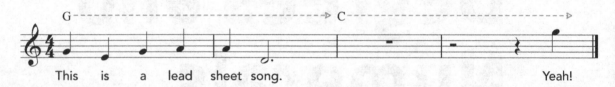

Melody

The melody is the notes on the staff.

Lyrics

Lyrics are the words of a song. Lyrics appear below the staff and line up with the melody and chords.

3 Steps to Know the Key of a Song

Every major and natural minor scale is related to a key, which is the summary of all the notes of the scale (remember the buckets?). When you write or perform music with a key signature you are "in" that key. All Level 1: Lead Sheet songs have two possible key signatures and two relative keys per key signature: C major/ A minor, and G major/E minor. Below is the formula to figure out the key of most songs!

> **1. Key Signature + 2. Chords + 3. Common Notes = Key of the Lead Sheet or Song**

53 **1. How to Identify the Key of a Lead Sheet: Key Signature**

Each key signature works with a relative major and natural minor scale. The symbol for each key is the same as the chord symbol for a triad.

> **Major keys: C, G   Minor keys: A-, E-**

No Accidentals: Key of C or A-

One Sharp: Key of G or E-

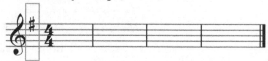

2. How to Identify the Key of a Lead Sheet: Chords

Chords are the first step to identifying the key of music. A chord progression is two or more chords played in a row. Use common chord progressions to quickly see if chords show a major key. Many songs are built using one or more chord progressions, and the chords repeat throughout the song.

I vi IV V Common Chord Progression 1:

Shows a Major Key

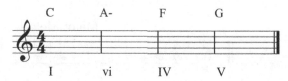

Some songs that use progression 1:

"I Will Always Love You"	Dolly Parton
"Perfect"	Ed Sheeran
"Baby"	Justin Bieber

I V vi IV Common Chord Progression 2:

Shows a Major Key

Some songs that use progression 2:

"Girls Like You"	Maroon 5
"Hey, Soul Sister"	Train
"So Lonely"	The Police

vi IV I V Common Chord Progression 3:

Shows a Major Key

Some songs that use progression 3:

"A New Day Has Come"	Celine Dion
"Apologize"	Timbaland
"Faded"	Alan Walker

How to Identify the Key of a Lead Sheet: Chords

1. Identify the major and minor key connected with the key signature of the music.

2. Make sure that all the chords belong in the key of the key signature. All the chords in the song should come from the harmonized scale of the key.

3. Major keys/progressions usually start on I, IV, or V. Minor keys usually start on i.

4. If the first and last chords are I or i of a key, it is likely that the song is in that key. If a song starts and ends on a G chord, it is likely in the key of G.

5. If there is no I chord, it is likely the music is in the relative minor key.

6. Many chord progressions have a I or i.

3. How to Identify the Key of a Lead Sheet: Common Notes

There are a few Common Notes that show if a song is in the major or relative minor key. Pay special attention to the notes that land on the strongest and strong beats of each measure, since the strongest and strong beats are more important in Western/European music culture.

Common Notes First Measures:

Melody:	Major: $\hat{1}$, $\hat{3}$, $\hat{5}$
	Minor: $\hat{1}$, $\flat\hat{3}$, $\hat{5}$

Common Notes Last Measures:

Melody:	Major: $\hat{1}$, $\hat{3}$, $\hat{5}$, $\hat{6}$, $\hat{7}$
	Minor: $\hat{1}$, $\flat\hat{3}$, $\hat{5}$

How to Identify the Key of a Lead sheet: Melody

1. Identify the major and minor key associated with the key signature of the music.

2. Analyze the notes of the melody for the first few measures and in the last few measures of the song as if the key is major and also as if the key is minor. Pay special attention to the notes that land on the strongest and strong beats.

3. If the notes in the first and last measures and especially on the strong beats include $\hat{1}$ of a scale, the song is usually in the key of that scale. You are looking for more major or minor Common Notes in the first few and last few measures.

Repeating $\hat{1}$ and $\hat{5}$ are clues this melody is minor. The $\hat{1}\hat{5}\hat{1}$ at the end is common in older genres.

Repeating $\hat{1}$ and $\hat{5}$ are clues this melody is major. The $\hat{1}$ + $\hat{5}$ are more important than $\hat{3}$ for deciding.

54 Chords + Melody

In modern music, **you may not find** $\hat{1}$ in the first few and last few measures for major and minor keys and melodies. In these cases you will need to look at the chords and the other Common Notes in the melody together to figure out if the melody is showing the major or relative minor key.

The example above is likely a major melody just looking at the scale degrees. However, there are no C chords (**I**) in the whole song. Even though the melody is showing minor Common Notes on weak beats, we can tell the key is minor because of the chords. It starts and ends on an A- (**i**).

3 Steps to Know the Key of a Song: Final Decision

To make a final decision on what key a written piece of music is in, ask yourself the following questions and think about the information below.

1. Key Signature: Major and Minor Keys

- There are 4 possible keys: C, G, A-, E-.

- What are the two possible keys that this song could be in?

- Looking at the key signature, which major key and minor key (they will always be relative major and minor) could you use? (C/A- or G/E-)

2. Chords: Chords and Chord Progressions

- Do the chords show a Common Chord Progression?

- Based on the key signature, is there a **I** or **i** chord in the music? If the key signature is for C/A- but there are no C or A- chords in the music, you will need to look at the melody.

- Do all the chords come from the harmonized scale that is the same name as the key?

- What are the first and last chords?

- Which chords are used the most?

- There can be minor chords in a major key and major chords in a minor key.

- If there are no or very few minor chords in the song, the key is probably major.

- If there are no or very few major chords in the song, the key is probably minor.

- Are the chords showing a major key or a minor key?

3. Melody: Common Notes and Strong Beats

- Are there major or minor Common Notes or $\hat{1}$ from one of the two possible relative keys on strongest and strong beats in the first few and last few measures?

- Think of the scale degrees in terms of the major key. Which scale degrees fall on the strongest and strong beats of the first few and last few measures?

- Think of the scale degrees in terms of the minor key. Which scale degrees fall on the strongest and strong beats of the first few and last few measures?

- Are the melody and common notes showing a major key or a minor key?

Key of the Song =

Chords/Progression = Major +	Common Notes = Major =	Major Key!
Chords/Progression = Can't Tell +	Common Notes = Major =	Major Key!
Chords/Progression = Minor +	Common Notes = Minor =	Minor Key!
Chords/Progression = Can't Tell +	Common Notes = Minor =	Minor Key!

How to Write an Analysis 1

55 How to Write the Key of a Piece of Music

After you figure out the key of a piece of music, it is time to write the key on the paper, or mark up a digital score. A "score" is a printed representation of music, which can be physical paper or a digital file on a phone, tablet, or other screen.

You have 2 key signatures and 4 possible keys that may show up for Level 1.

Major Keys: C: G: Minor Keys: A-: E-:

> **1.** Write the letter name of the key below the clef in the first measure of the music.
>
> **2.** Write the quality of the key: blank for major, minus sign for minor.
>
> **3.** Write a colon.

Example: Scarborough Fair

How to Write a Scale Degree Analysis

1. Write "SD" and the key + colon below the staff. Major Keys: C: G: Minor Keys: A-: E-:

2. Write scale degrees below the staff under each note that is an attack in the piece of music (not the second note of a tie).

3. If there is a note that is one half-step lower than where it would be in the major scale, the scale degree gets a ♭ accidental. Example: ♭$\hat{3}$.

4. If there is a note that is one half-step higher than where it would be in the major scale, the scale degree gets a # accidental. Example: #$\hat{4}$.

5. Add a ♭ to ♭$\hat{3}$ ♭$\hat{6}$ ♭$\hat{7}$ if you are writing a scale degree analysis in a minor key.

6. If ♭$\hat{3}$ ♭$\hat{6}$ or ♭$\hat{7}$ is raised up a half step from the natural minor scale, remove the ♭ accidental from the scale degree.

1.

SD G:

2.

(D) (G)

Ba - by shark, doo doo doo doo___ doo doo

SD G: $\hat{5}$ $\hat{6}$ $\hat{1}$ $\hat{1}$ $\hat{1}$ $\hat{1}$ $\hat{1}$ $\hat{1}$ $\hat{1}$

Example: Scarborough Fair

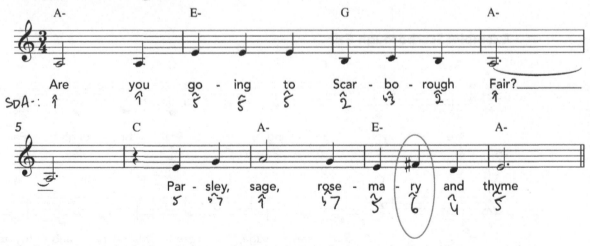

56 In m.8 there is a scale degree that is not from the A natural minor scale. Do not let a non-scale or non-key note stop you from figuring out the key. If 95% of the notes are in the key of the key signature, you are good to go! There is no ♭ accidental before $\hat{6}$ in m. 8. See Rule 6. at the top of this page!

How to Write a Roman Numeral (Harmonic) Analysis

1. Write the key + colon again below "SD (key): " Major Keys: C: G: Minor Keys: A-: E-:

2. Write one Roman Numeral directly under each chord symbol in the lead sheet or song. Write the Roman Numerals below the staff and below the scale degrees for all chords.

- In the key of G: a "G" chord is **I**. In the key of E-: a "G" chord is **III**. In the key of C: a "G" chord is **V**. In the key of A-: a "G" chord is **VII**.

- The Roman Numerals should show how the chord symbol relates to the scale of the key. Roman Numeral I or i for scale degree 1, RN II or ii for scale degree 2, and so on.

- Show the quality of the chord: Major = **I II III IV V VI VII**, Minor = **i ii iii iv v vi vii**

1.

2.

Example: Scarborough Fair

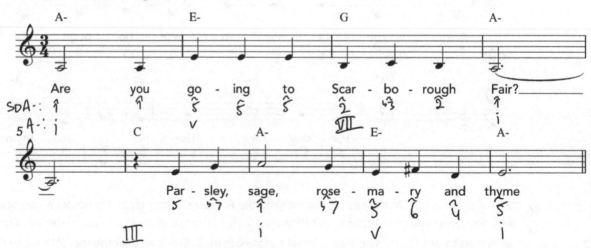

Scale Degree + Harmonic Analysis Example: Baby Shark

Baby Shark

Music: Traditional American Campfire Songs
Words: Traditional American Campfire Songs
Arrangement by Best Music Coach & Dan Spencer

Level 1: Leadsheet

Now you can analyze all the
Level 1: Lead Sheet songs!
www.bestsheetmusic.com

Review: Analysis 1

- How to analyze lead sheets
- How to read lead sheets
    Chords
    Melody
    Lyrics

- 3 steps to identify a lead sheet or song
    Key signature
    Chords
    Common notes

- How to identify the key of a lead sheet: key signature
- How to identify the key of a lead sheet: chords
- How to identify the key of a lead sheet: common notes
- How to identify the key of a lead sheet: final decision
- How to write an analysis 1
    How to write the key of a piece of music
    How to write a scale degree analysis
    How to write a Roman Numeral analysis

What's Next?

1. Complete your *Best Music Theory Workbook for Beginners 1*!

2. Analyze 5-10 Level 1: Lead Sheet songs from bestsheetmusic.com

Level 2

In the next book, *The Music Theory Book for Beginners: 2*, you will learn so much more cool and applicable theory so you can understand even more music and take your playing, singing, writing, composing, songwriting, producing, or music appreciation to the next level!

Write Music 1: Use What You Know

Use everything you have learned so far in this book to compose music and write songs!

How to Write Compositions 1

1. Pick a major or minor key.

2. Use the scale from that key for the melody of the song or composition.

3. Harmonize the scale and write down the 6 possible chords you can use for the scale on a separate sheet of paper or note application on a device.

4. Combine scale notes with different rhythms and rests to create the melody.

5. (Optional) Add words to your melody under the melody notes below the staff. Line each word up with a note, or split words across more than one note by using hyphens.

6. Pick different combinations of chords from the harmonized scale to go with the melody.

You can follow this six-step process by:

1. Writing out the notes of the melody and adding the chords above the staff to create a lead sheet. This is a good option if you can play an instrument, so you can hear what your music sounds like.

2. Write the triads (chords) and melody out on two separate staves in a music notation software or digital audio workstation (DAW). You will need 2 instruments/staves/tracks so you can hear them BOTH at the same time. When you see a vertical line connecting the staves, that shows you both staves will sound at the same time.

3. You can change the rhythm of the chords using everything you have learned.

1.

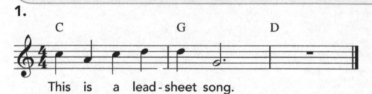

2.

3.

More Common Chord Progressions

Try out all of the chord progressions below with 1 chord per measure for 4 measures, then repeat the chord progression over and over again until your song is done. Change the last chord of the piece to the chord that is the tonic of the key to bring things home.

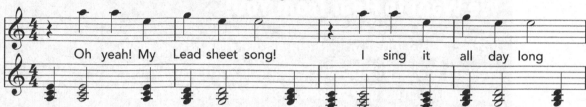

Write the triads to be lower than the melody to help the melody notes stand out.

Common Chord Progressions: Major Keys

Each chord lasts for 1 measure in any time signature.

- I IV V V
- I I IV V
- I IV I V
- I IV V IV
- I vi IV V
- I vi ii V
- **Make up your own!**

Common Chord Progressions: Minor Keys

Each chord lasts for 1 measure in any time signature.

- i VII VI VII
- i VI III VII
- i iv v i
- i iv VII i
- i i VI VII
- i VI VI VII
- **Make up your own!**

Learn how to write words to songs and how to craft beautiful melodies in books 2-3!

learn the rules, follow the rules, break the rules, make music. the music in your heart may not conform to the rules you will learn in this book, or it may follow the rules without exception. rules provide a structure to be creative within. all ways of making music are fine. go make music and express yourself with passion.

We Want to Hear from You!

Let us know what you think about this book, how we can make this book better for you, and what else you would like to see from Best Music Coach!

publishing@bestmusiccoach.com

www.bestmusiccoach.com

facebook.com/bestmusiccoach

youtube.com/bestmusiccoach

twitter.com/bestmusiccoach

instagram.com/bestmusiccoach

Acknowledgments

Thank you to my dear students, Derek, Lauren, Anakin, Matthew, Dipti, Kindra, Corrine, and Rozlind for your help in pacing this book and for your collective cognitive bravery to take on much more complex and larger theory tasks and concepts than presented herein.

Thank you Jasara for your radical support.

Sources:

Many of the rules for engraving in this book can be traced directly to *Behind Bars: The Definitive Guide to Music Notation* by Elaine Gould. ISBN: 978-0571514564